DOUBLE TALK

DOUBLE TALK

*Bilingualism and the Politics
of Ethnicity in Catalonia*

Kathryn A. Woolard

STANFORD UNIVERSITY PRESS
Stanford, California

Stanford University Press
Stanford, California
© 1989 by the Board of Trustees of the
Leland Stanford Junior University
Printed in the United States of America

CIP data appear at the end of the book

Published with the assistance of the
University of Pennsylvania Research Foundation

To my mother and father

PREFACE

Though this book concerns general, enduring questions about bilingual life, it concentrates on a particular period in the recent history of Catalonia. The year that my fieldwork was done, 1979–80, marked a turning point in the political development of the community. In a referendum of October 1979, voters approved a Statute of Autonomy, giving Catalonia a degree of home rule as an "autonomous community." In the spring, people went to the polls again, to elect a Catalan government for the first time in some forty years.

Catalonia has changed since I did my fieldwork. Though it has developed fitfully, the autonomous institutional structure that was mandated in 1979 is now nearly fully in place, and the Catalan government for several years has been setting and implementing policy in important areas such as education. A law of "linguistic normalization" was passed in 1983, a Catalan television channel was established the same year, and language policy, especially in schooling, has evolved. New Catalan street signs and new street names bear witness to these changes.

The same nationalist party that was elected in 1980 has grown in strength and retains the Catalan presidency, but the political framework surrounding it in the Spanish state has changed considerably.

Whereas in 1979 conservatives with links to Franco still headed the Spanish government, the Socialists have governed since 1982. Political parties that were important players on the regional or state scene of 1980, such as the Communist party and its Catalan affiliate, have since withered, split, and in some cases been reincarnated.

This book makes no pretense of presenting an up-to-the-minute journalistic account of the situation of Barcelona, Catalonia, or Spain. Rather, I intend the ethnographic portrait I draw to be specific to the eventful year that I witnessed, and I have introduced a minimal amount of data from later than 1980. It is my belief—certainly my hope—that the inevitable flow of history does not mean that my research and my findings are no longer of interest. If anything, the continued existence and evolution of democratic Spain and autonomous Catalonia should render this work even more relevant.

What follows is an analysis of the meanings and uses of language and ethnicity in Catalonia at a political turning point. For those who know and care about Spain or Catalonia (or both), such a portrait should provide insight into the developments of the time and some that have occurred since. For sociolinguists, anthropologists, political scientists, and sociologists approaching this case study from a theoretical interest in bilingualism or ethnicity, the precise dates of my fieldwork are of course of less concern. The analysis suggests principles of language values, linguistic attitudes, and bilingual behavior that, although situated historically, are intended to have more general validity.

Some terminological and stylistic points need to be clarified. "Nation" is a word mired in political assumptions in Western usage, and it can be a fighting word in Spain. Generally in this book, the words "nation" and "nationalism" will refer not to Spain but to the sentimental community of Catalonia and Catalanism. Though Catalonia is the "nation" in question, "state" will refer (except where noted in Chap. 3) to the central Spanish state, which occasionally also appears as "Madrid" or "Castile." Although most Catalans reject the term "region" in reference to Catalonia, I will use it on occasion when I want to stress the structural position of Catalonia within a larger political unit. But my use of the term implies no comment on the validity of Catalonia's claim to nationhood. The word "immigrants" in reference to Spaniards who have come to Catalonia sometimes puzzles those readers who prefer "migration" for movement within a political state. But "immigration" is the term used in Catalonia and thus in this book, and it emphasizes the political and social importance of national as well as state boundaries in the movement of human groups. Since the Spanish language is generally known as "Castilian" in Iberia, that term is used in this work.

All the personal names given in this work are pseudonyms, even when only first names are used. In some cases I have changed incidental details of individuals' biographies in order to protect them from recognition by other Catalan readers of this book.

Although I often refer to Catalonia and Catalans, the sociolinguistic commentary here should be thought of as applying only to the Barcelona metropolitan area; linguistic attitudes and behavior may differ considerably in the provinces and in rural areas in particular. Even more important, I find I have often been unable to resist the ethnographic present tense when writing about general norms of ethnic identification or language use. But that should be looked upon as no more than a stylistic convention, for the generalizations proposed are meant to be true only of 1979–80, and language etiquette and perhaps even principles of identification may well have changed since then. Finally, I will introduce native terms in Catalan unless Castilian is more relevant to the point. Catalan lexical items will be given in boldface type (e.g. **ànima**); Catalan and Castilian personal names, place names, and proper nouns will be given in roman type (e.g. Partit); and Castilian lexical items will be *italicized*. No distinction between Catalan and Castilian is made in book or other conventionally italicized titles.

A few comments should be made about how this study was done. The research environment and the scope of my questions necessitated methodological eclecticism. Most urban ethnographies have focused on small, well-defined subcommunities or marginal groups within the city—"urban villagers" (Gans 1962)—rather than on the complexity of relations between different sectors of a city's population. Successful urban ethnographies often depend on the very marginality of the group studied, since informants not participating fully in the institutions of the larger society can grant a trusted ethnographer greater access to more domains of their lives. Another tactic of urban ethnographers has been to focus on only one domain of social activity, such as family life or school. In spite of advances in the adaptation of traditional field techniques to new settings, we have not yet achieved the same kind of holistic description of urban life as is expected in ethnographies of simpler societies.

Anthropologists have often focused on stable and unconscious social processes. As we move into the study of conflict in modern complex society, we must come to terms with the highly politicized character of our research problems. The political nature of research itself becomes clearer than ever, with both positive and negative consequences for the study. On the one hand, there is no difficulty in getting people to talk about the topics of language and ethnicity in Barcelona. But on the other hand, there is a heavy layer of conscious, received political ideology—expressions of what *ought* to be the case—coating more quotidian attitudes and behaviors.

For all these reasons, I found it useful to piece together a variety of evidence culled from a spectrum of informants through a number of techniques. Five basic kinds of data provide the foundation for my analysis: (1) observation of formally organized political events; (2) printed materials gathered daily from periodicals; (3) observation of everyday language and interactional behavior, backed by limited recording of natural discourse; (4) interviews and organized discussions about language and ethnic identity, usually tape-recorded, as well as numerous unrecorded spontaneous discussions; and (5) a quasi-experimental measure of language attitudes.

Rather than a single stable sample, I worked with a variety of informants who might be arranged in concentric circles by degree of acquaintance. I developed perhaps half a dozen key, close relationships, and regular relations with another thirty or so people. Most, though not all, of the people in these two inner circles were between the ages of twenty-five and forty; it is probably quite significant to my analysis that they were often people whom I felt to be "like me" in important ways. Their spontaneous discussions contributed substantially to my understanding. My key relationships leaned toward a single political persuasion, the "progressives" of the Catalan Communist Party (Partit Socialista Unificat de Catalunya). Though this may have biased my view of the situation in some respects, none of my informants would claim or should be burdened with responsibility for my views.

Beyond these two groups of informants lay another circle of about 50 people I met with more than once but on an irregular basis; this circle was diverse in political, linguistic, and class background, as well as in age. I used both the Catalan and the Castilian language in my formal and informal interviews and discussions, depending largely on my interlocutor's choice (although, early in my work, my inadequate control of Catalan forced the choice at times). In most cases my first introduction was as a friend of a friend; it was only to the students who participated in my formal experimental measure that I was presented primarily as a researcher.

Those approximately 250 experimental respondents form the next circle of contact; with about 50 of these I developed a more extensive relationship, returning for informal discussions and interviews, and in some cases maintaining further personal contact. Finally, beyond this group are the hundreds of residents of Barcelona with whom I shared a socially defined space or interacted perhaps once, some intensively in friendly circumstances, some in fleeting business transactions, but all of whom provided me with insights into the linguistic and social norms of life in Barcelona.

In addition to these invaluable informants who through custom and good sense must remain anonymous, many people are to be thanked for many different kinds of assistance. The Social Science Research Council and the American Council of Learned Societies granted the fellowship that made this fieldwork possible. All the conclusions and opinions expressed are my own and not necessarily those of the Councils. The Department of Anthropology at the University of California, Berkeley, and the Research Foundation of the University of Pennsylvania provided additional financial support for this project.

For assistance in the field, my thanks to Helena Calsamiglia, Santiago Costa, Valeria Salcioli, Luís Paniello, Helena Rotés, Lluís Riera, Claudi Esteva Fabregat, and Lluís V. Aracil, and especially to Amparo Tuson. Thanks, also, for indispensable assistance with the statistical analysis, to Jim Boster. I am grateful to John Gumperz, Eugene Hammel, and Susan Ervin-Tripp for guiding this work as a dissertation, and to others who read and advised at various stages: Burton Benedict, Elizabeth Colson, fellow students in the dissertation seminar at Berkeley, 1981, Susan DiGiacomo, Gary McDonogh, Jim Amelang, Maite Turell, Miquel Strubell, and especially Susan Gal and Juan Linz. For assistance in preparing versions of the manuscript, I thank Susanna Fosch, Yoko Koike Johanning, Chérie Francis, and Dory Lightfoot. For all kinds of help along the way, thanks to Mike Agar, Lisa Warantz, Susan Niles, Bambi Schieffelin, Buck Schieffelin, Helena Ramos, and Joel Sobel.

I am grateful to the Patronat Municipal de Turisme de Barcelona for providing me with the city photographs, nos. 1 and 11, in the section following page 72; and to Montserrat Manet for allowing me to use her photograph of Gaudí's Casa Milà, no. 12.

K. A. W.

CONTENTS

Six pages of pictures follow page 72

DOUBLE TALK

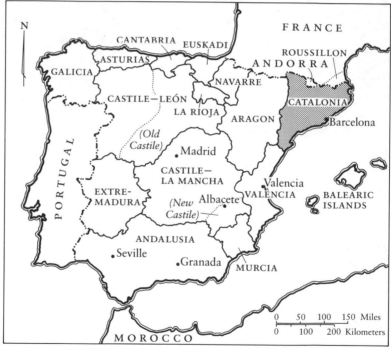

Regions of Peninsular Spain (traditional regional names are shown in parentheses). The Catalan-speaking areas ("El Països Catalans") are Catalonia, Valencia, and the Balearic Islands (Spain); Roussillon (France); Andorra; and the city of Alguer in Sardinia.

CHAPTER ONE |||| INTRODUCTION

This is a study of the politics of language and ethnicity in a modern
industrial city. The city is Barcelona, the capital of Catalonia, historically a distinct polity and now an autonomous political community within Spain. The central questions addressed in this book
concern the values and uses of the two languages, Catalan and Castilian, that coexist in this community.

In Barcelona, as in many other parts of the world, language is a
key symbol of ethnic identity, a marker that summarizes a number
of perceived differences between groups of people (Ortner 1973). As
such, it has served for the past century as a prime symbolic resource
of Catalan nationalism. Language and ethnicity are highly ideolog-
ized and controversial in Barcelona, playing a critical role not only in
the social and political organization of the city and the autonomous
community that it leads, but in the restructuring of the post-Franco
Spanish state as well. More than just a study of a sociolinguistic situation per se, then, this book is intended to contribute to our understanding of the relation between cultural practices and political possibilities within the modern state.

Although the events observed and documented here all occur
within Barcelona, they respond to forces, both historical and contem-

porary, originating well beyond the boundaries of Catalonia. There is growing recognition in anthropology of the desirability, as well as the difficulty, of identifying the linkages between everyday behaviors in the face-to-face communities traditionally studied and the institutions and conflicting forces of the wider social system in which such communities are embedded. Toward this end, two different senses of "political" activity are of concern in this book: formal politics, encompassing the actions of political parties and organized interest groups in competition for access to power within the state; and interpersonal politics, or the negotiation of relations of dominance and solidarity between individuals in interaction. The goal of this dual approach is to understand the relationship between the public and personal meanings of the linguistic practices that fire Catalan nationalism.

Catalonia is something of an anomaly among minority regions in centralized states. Although it is a periphery that has long suffered political subordination and cultural and linguistic domination by the Castilian center, it has not experienced the economic underdevelopment that typifies such regions (see, for example, Hechter 1975). On the contrary, Catalonia was a leader in introducing a bourgeois social order based on industrial capitalism, and in this regard most of Spain lagged significantly behind. Catalonia has long been one of the richest and most developed areas of the Spanish state, and in 1978, the year before this study began, it had more industries and more real wealth than any other region (Taylor 1983: vi; cf. Linz and de Miguel 1966, Linz 1973). Metallurgy, chemicals, and textiles are the major industries, and less than 7 percent of the labor force is employed in agriculture (Caraben Ribó 1982: 82).

Catalonia's early economic lead over the rest of Spain gave rise to a second phenomenon unusual in a minority region: a primarily nonnative working class. To fill the need for manual labor in expanding industries, Castilian-speaking workers, primarily from the impoverished south of Spain, immigrated to Catalonia in a flow that began in the 1920's and became torrential by the 1960's. While the total population of Spain increased by 50 percent between 1940 and 1980, that of Catalonia increased by 110 percent. The destination of the vast majority of immigrants was Barcelona. With some 1,750,000 inhabitants confined between a mountain and the Mediterranean, contemporary Barcelona's population density is four times that of

Madrid (ibid.). The city was saturated early, and growth from immigration shifted to the satellite cities, some with populations as large as 300,000, that now form a belt around the capital. Over 4,000,000 people live in the Barcelona metropolitan area (Recolons et al. 1979: 36).

These immigrants and their descendants now constitute nearly half of the Catalonian population. The Catalans themselves are an unusual territorial-based minority, since they form the greater part of the propertied, managerial, and professional sectors of their community, with economic power over laborers speaking a dialect of the language the central state has attempted to impose from above.

The historical separation of political and economic dominance in Catalonia allows us to consider the relative effects of these two forces on sociolinguistic and ethnic phenomena. Two very different kinds of ethnolinguistic "minorities" are of concern in this study: Catalans and Catalonia within the Spanish state, and immigrant-origin Castilian speakers within Catalonia. The ethnographic focus is the description of the boundaries and relations between these social groups in Barcelona as they are marked and managed by language use.

Language Choice: Some Theoretical Issues

Some of the key questions in work on bilingual societies are about patterns of language acquisition and language maintenance or loss. Who learns which language, and under what conditions does one language displace another? The underlying concern is *why*: why are some people able to retain a minority language while other groups lose theirs? why are some groups slower and less successful in acquiring a majority language? We look to social facts to explain linguistic facts.

For Barcelona, there are two overriding sociolinguistic questions: why the Catalan language has survived as long and well as it has, and whether it will survive longer. The first question turns primarily on the behavior of autochthonous, native-speaking Catalans, but the second depends equally on the linguistic choices made by the many Castilian speakers of immigrant origins.

The contemporary vitality of Catalan as a vernacular language despite centuries of institutional inferiority is unique among the minority languages of western Europe, and especially noteworthy in

light of the repression of the Franco years. Sociolinguists have invoked the Catalan case as a counterexample to the generalization
that minority languages erode in complex industrialized societies
(Fishman 1964, Ryan 1979, Milroy 1980). For outside observers in
particular, the remarkable fact in need of explanation has been that
Catalan is so tenaciously maintained despite the institutional power
and prestige, not to mention worldwide utility, of Castilian.

Native sociolinguistic commentators, both amateur and professional, are more caught up in the second question, and in the doubt
whether this apparently remarkable situation can continue. With
approximately half the Catalan population now of immigrant,
Castilian-speaking origin or descent, the critical issues concern the
acquisition of Catalan as a second language, rather than just its continued maintenance as a mother tongue. What conditions encourage
immigrants and their children to learn Catalan, and under what conditions is such learning constrained? If learned, in what circumstances will Catalan actually be used by those of Castilian-speaking
origins? And, most pragmatically, can language planners and poli-
cymakers alter circumstances to encourage such acquisition and use?

The ethnographic and experimental methods used here are aimed
at discovering what it means, in several senses and in various circumstances, for a person to speak Catalan. Most obviously in question
is what actual linguistic practices characterize the bilingual Catalan
speaker. But beyond this is the meaning of choice between Catalan
and Castilian in face-to-face interaction, that is, its effects on social
relations. A third question is what it means to a Castilian speaker to
learn Catalan: what are the incentives and costs, the personal transformation, that might be entailed? And finally, what might immigrant attitudes toward the Catalan language mean for the political
future of the Catalan community? These are the issues explored in
this work.

In the search for generalizations about the loss or maintenance of
minority languages, theorists have considered a variety of factors:
type of contact setting, functional distribution of the languages, economic development and industrialization, degree of political participation (e.g. Weinreich 1974, Fishman 1964, Stewart 1968, Lewis
1978, Deutsch 1966). In more recent work, researchers have turned
their attention to variables that link these macrosociological factors
to individuals' decisions. The interest is in knowing *how* such large-

scale developments affect actual language behavior (Gal 1979, Woolard 1989), and thus in accounting for anomalous cases as well as those that fit the general patterns. Motivated by this interest, the present work investigates extensively the symbolic values that attach to the two languages and mediate between structural changes and individual choices.

The symbolic value of language choice has figured in the explanations developed by a variety of disciplines for language maintenance, shift, acquisition, and codeswitching; linguists, anthropologists, and social psychologists have often made language values central to their analyses. From this cumulative attention, two distinct and often conflicting kinds of social values have been conceptualized as attaching to (i.e., both reflected in and enacted by) language choice. Many labels exist for these two concepts, but they are usually conceived as two independent axes governing social relations as well as language use.

The first, which can be visualized as a vertical axis, has been most often discussed as prestige, but is variously known as dominance, power, status, instrumental motivation, or negative face (White 1980, Brown and Gilman 1960, Milroy 1980, Weinreich 1974, Gal 1979, Dorian 1981, Gardner and Lambert 1972, Brown and Levinson 1978). The second, the horizontal axis, is more unanimously labeled solidarity, although it has also been called covert prestige, social bonding, positive face, and integrative motivation (Labov 1966b, Trudgill 1972, Dorian 1981, Brown and Levinson 1978, Gardner and Lambert 1972).

The contrast between solidarity and some notion of dominance has intuitive appeal and has been of considerable utility in explaining many minority-language patterns. However, in some senses this dichotomous distinction is an oversimplification that conflates important factors. The concept of prestige in particular has been recognized as problematic, and Fishman has noted that it is easily discredited unless serious qualifications and redefinitions are attempted (1964: 55). The failure of general theories of prestige to account for particular instances of linguistic behavior has been pointed out, with Catalan as a prime example (ibid., Weinreich 1974).

The very slippage of terminology, especially in reference to the vertical axis, demonstrates that there are some further analytical distinctions to be made if we are going to answer such questions as,

"Why do low-prestige languages persist?" (Ryan 1979). More than simply identifying a competing value such as solidarity, we must get a better grasp on the concept of language prestige itself, and its relation to various forms of dominance in human social organization. The core of this study, presented in Chapter 5, explores precisely this problem, in an effort not simply to describe correctly the language situation in Catalonia but as a step in the clarification of language values and their relation to language behavior.

Ethnicity and Nationalism: Some Theoretical Considerations

In western tradition since the Romantic period, consideration of the symbolic value of language, and of solidarity values in particular, leads directly to issues of ethnic identity. For a period of about ten to fifteen years beginning in the mid-1960's, social-scientific and particularly anthropological studies of ethnicity and minority nationalism multiplied rapidly. The sudden increase in attention was triggered both by internal developments in the discipline and by "real world" events. Within anthropology, a shift in focus from stable corporate groups to more fluid social networks and voluntary associations, from structure to process, and from relatively homogeneous to complex societies created the theoretical context for the study of ethnicity. In the larger world, many western polities were surprised by an apparently sudden eruption of ethnic movements and minority nationalisms, a development that seemed to beg for social-scientific explanation.

The tone of world events is now changing, with a mainstream nationalism, even xenophobia, growing to match and counter the minority movements and immigrant concerns in many western nations, such as the United States and France. The social-scientific interest in understanding ethnic phenomena seems to have ebbed earlier and at an even faster rate. Although this is the predictable fate of any intellectual fashion—the moving academic hand, having writ, moves on—it is marked in this case by considerable theoretical disarray, a sensation that ethnicity has become tiresome not because we have solved all its puzzles, but because we are no longer sure what kind of puzzles these are. Although a wealth of research material on ethnicity and the "new" nationalisms appeared in a relatively short time, a coherent account of ethnicity has been more recalcitrant in emerging.

One reason for, or perhaps one facet of, this failure is that the very definition of "ethnicity" itself proved difficult to agree upon. Little consensus has been achieved about the appropriate understanding of the location of ethnic experience in human life, and thus about the level of scientific abstraction on which to address it. Ethnicity all too obviously is manifested in and reverberates through many spheres: the intimate realm of the individual's sense of self, the daily processes of face-to-face interaction, the ties of friendship and neighborhood, the formal organization of brotherhoods and parties, separatist groups and warfare. Correspondingly, considerable variation exists in diagnoses of the "real" locus of ethnicity: in the individual psyche (Isaacs 1975, Novak 1980), in group experiences of economic subordination (Hechter 1975) or competition for resources (Despres 1975a, 1975b, Cohen 1974b), or in an ideological superstructure (Fox, Aull, and Cimino 1978).

When viewed as a "primordial sentiment" (Shils 1957, cf. Geertz 1973), or as an aboriginal property of the "folk," ethnicity is often characterized as a conservative and backward-looking basis for personal identity and political community (DeVos 1975). An important corrective to this view was the recognition that ethnicity is not always the survival of cultural diversity born of geographical and social isolation, but may be the outcome of intensive interaction, a constellation of practices that evolve to channel complex social relations (Barth 1969, Cohen 1974a, 1974b, Brown and Levinson 1979). From a related perspective, then, politicized manifestations of ethnicity are not a reflex of conservatism or a retreat to outmoded political forms, but modern innovations and adaptations to contemporary political institutions (Fox, Aull, and Cimino 1978).

If primordialist approaches to the topic focus too narrowly on the individual or the folk, the contrasting view of ethnicity as a secondary construct, an epiphenomenal reflex of economic or political interest, is too often accompanied by a nearly exclusive attention to elites. The researcher who presents ethnicity principally as a political tool created and manipulated by elites often skirts the important question of why the "masses" are persuaded to identify their interests with those of the political elite. A split portrait emerges, of leaders on the one hand as willful actors capable of calculating benefits and negotiating gains, and of the popular classes on the other hand as cultural automatons, blindly responding to manipulated symbols. It is indeed appropriate to view elites as commanding more information for the planning of strategies, and more resources to put them into action, but a social phenomenon like ethnic nationalism that depends on the actions of both elite and popular classes cannot be explained fully from the perspective of only one of these segments of society.

The political appeal of particular sets of symbols is constrained by the experience of ethnicity as it organizes daily life. In turn, the received, publicly mediated meanings of group membership inexorably affect the individual's daily experience of that identity. As Moore points out, changes in the relative position of individuals and changes in social regularities are connected though not coextensive phenomena (1975: 229). The position taken in this book is that we must see ethnic phenomena in the different contexts of individual and group experience neither as more or less real, nor as isomorphic, but rather as reflecting back on and constraining one another, often in a process of increasing differentiation of social groups. Ethnicity is not a primordial but an emergent phenomenon, growing out of the interaction of social beings in a political and economic context. The interplay of different aspects of life organized by ethnicity—psychological, social, political—is not a distracting complication but rather the central focus of interest here as we look at the complex relations of Catalans and Castilians in Barcelona.

A second reason why ethnicity has escaped simple summation (while falling prey to simplistic statement) is precisely that it is a modern political phenomenon and occurs in complex societies. The utility of key symbols has often been found in the fact that they stand ambiguously for a multiplicity of meanings, and that through the mystification that symbols create, social contradictions can be resolved and conflicting interests harmonized (Cohen 1974a). In more complex societies, such consensus among the various segments of society sometimes may be more elusive (McDonogh 1986b). We find in societies such as Barcelona that "key symbols can provide the means through which different groups in the population may meaningfully disagree, rather than the means for them to reach consensus" (ibid.). Verdery, for example, shows how the ideology of nationalism in Romania began "as a way of describing difficult problems, as understood by those who wanted to argue about them with others" (1983: 353). We will see that such is the case with language in Barcelona; it is as much a symbol that expresses conflict and serves as a focus for disagreement as it is one that enables harmonious action.

A final reason why ethnicity, particularly ethnic politics, has proved conceptually troublesome is that what is often apprehended as a single process under a single rubric actually comprises several distinct processes, and the nature of the phenomenon to be described may change radically from phase to phase. Fredrik Barth has likened the diachronic study of ethnicity to the observation of an aquarium.* After examining a small fish in the window before us, studying its form and coloration, we may turn our gaze away for a moment. Upon turning back, we find ourselves face to face with a man-eating shark. If we seek to explain how the small fish grew to be such a large and dangerous one, we are bound to be mistaken. To look at different stages in an ethnic conflict as one continuous event is often to study the growth of the small fish into the shark; we must consider the possibility that the scene has changed, and that we are looking at a different creature.

The same ethnic symbols may be used to organize different segments of society and to articulate different conflicts at different times. Thus Catalanism in its different incarnations over the past century has variously expressed chiefly the interests of the upper bourgeoisie, the lower bourgeoisie, and the progressives of the professional classes. In each new incarnation, however, ethnic symbols may retain something of the symbolic load they once carried; thus we will find that at one and the same time the current Catalanist movement is charged with the bourgeois stereotypes of its early appearance and the anti-fascist leftism of the Civil War and Franco period.

Even within one particular incarnation of an ethnic movement, several different and even contradictory processes are involved. Looking at nationalist movements in the new states that have developed from former colonial territories, Geertz identified four distinct phases falling into two main categories: the process of triumphing over the colonial power, and the organization and stabilization of the

*Professor Barth developed this analogy in a class lecture given at the University of California, Berkeley, in the spring of 1981.

new state from the heterogeneous society out of which it developed. In each stage, the frame of self-perception, for knowing who we are, is revised. For all their intimate interconnections, anticolonialism (defining who we are not) is not the same as collective redefinition (defining who we are) (Geertz 1973: 238–39).

A nation-state is both an ethnic and a political community, but the confluence of the two is not a natural or necessary fact.* Coincidence between the nation and the state arises from deliberate political action, but that action may proceed in two directions. The state, defined by its administrative apparatus, may become or drive toward becoming a nation-state by promulgating a single language, a single culture, and a single set of symbols for the people within its borders; Grillo refers to this as the "ethnicization of the polity" (1980: 7). In this process, a self-conscious social and cultural community is created within political boundaries, in distinction to others outside the boundaries.

A nation, by contrast, seeks to become a nation-state through what Grillo (ibid.) calls the "politicization of ethnicity," agitating for a political apparatus to match its cultural boundaries. In this process, local sentiments and group solidarity are capitalized on and given a political cast. We will find that the crux of the political problem for autonomous Catalonia is that regional leaders are simultaneously and paradoxically engaged in these two contrary processes of nation-state building.

Though the current Catalanist phenomenon is not the same as its late-nineteenth- and early-twentieth-century incarnations, it draws on an ideological schema, an interpretive agenda made available in that period, one that over time, especially under the Franco regime, gained considerable power. The point of what follows in this book is not to explain the origins of ethnic sentiment in general, or the causes of Catalan nationalism in particular, but rather to look at the *functioning* of that ethnic sentiment: how it is articulated, and how it articulates a variety of experiences, in a particular and crucial period in the development of Catalan political and social relations within the Spanish state. If there is some conceptual gain in our thinking

*Within the extensive literature on this topic, see for example Fishman 1972b, Grillo 1980, Rokkan 1972. But see Tilly 1975 and Orridge 1982 for cautionary notes about the teleological assumptions often built into facile uses of the nation- and state-building concepts, a danger in this brief sketch.

about ethnicity to be found in this study, it lies in the insistence on viewing, on the one hand, nationalist politics through the lens of individual and small-group experiences, and, on the other, individual experience within the frame of larger political processes. The problematic relation between public ideology and everyday cultural practice is at the heart of this inquiry.

CHAPTER TWO CATALAN LANGUAGE
AND SOCIETY:
SOME HISTORICAL
NOTES

Although Catalan nationalist sentiment first appeared as a political
force in the nineteenth century, the Catalan struggle against Castilian
domination within the Spanish state is rooted centuries-deep in social and economic differences, as well as cultural and linguistic differences. The basic tension was that between an early-developing,
urban-industrial, bourgeois society, Catalonia, and an agrarian-
based, aristocratic oligarchy, Castile. Early structural differences not
only explain much of the conflict between Catalonia and the Spanish
state, they also provide the source and symbols of nationalist ideology, and a charter for modern Catalanism. For these reasons, a brief
outline of the historical development of Catalonia and the Catalan
language will be given here, emphasizing those periods and events
that have held the most symbolic power for the contemporary movement.

The Origins of the Catalan Language

A member of the Romance language family, Catalan is spoken
not only in Catalonia, but in Valencia and the Balearic Islands (Mallorca, Minorca, and Eivissa [Ibiza]) within Spain. It is also the official language of the small Pyrenean country of Andorra, and the tra-

ditional language of the French Roussillon (now the Department of Pyrénées-Orientales) and the city of Alguer in Sardinia.

The territory that is modern Catalonia was ruled by Rome as part of the province of Tarraconensis from the third century B.C. until the fifth century A.D. Owing to the dynamics of the later reconquest of the Iberian peninsula from Arab rule, the geographical distribution of the modern Catalan-speaking region reflects the boundaries of the medieval polities more than those of this early Roman administrative unit.

Nonetheless, the linguistic differentiation of Catalan and Provençal, on the one hand, from Castilian and Portuguese, on the other, has been attributed to the slower Roman colonization of the coastal region than of the interior territories of Iberia, and to the closer linkage of the port of Tarragona to Rome throughout the period of domination. Because of continued contact and interchange with Rome, Catalan developed from a more modern and more popular form of Latin than did Castilian, evolving in the southern and interior Roman province of Baetica (Sanchis Guarner 1980: 12–14, Veny 1986: 14–15).

Romance scholars do not question the status of Catalan as an independent language, but the combined effects of limited territorial extension, official repression, and policies of "dialectalization" (Kloss 1967a) have created a common popular impression that Catalan is a dialect of Spanish. Linguists do not agree on a technical definition of a language as opposed to a dialect, and the distinction is as often political as linguistic (Gumperz 1972). One facetious definition of a language relevant in the Catalonian case is "a dialect with an army."

In strictly linguistic terms, then, it is not of interest to insist on the status of Catalan as a language. To avert common misconceptions, however, it is important to do so, since Catalan fits none of the usual definitions of a dialect. Mutual intelligibility is the most frequent criterion of a dialectal relation, and Catalan is not mutually intelligible with Castilian. Catalan did not derive from Castilian, but has its own parallel developmental history, closely linked to that of Provençal, and an autonomous grammatical system and lexicon. Nor is Catalan simply an oral vernacular; it has a distinct literary standard and an early and extensive history of literary use. Catalan is, in Kloss's (1967b) typology, an *abstand* language (language by distance) rather than a dialect or an *ausbau* language (language by elaboration).

Arab commentators in the ninth century noted a distinct Romance vernacular in the territory from Barcelona to Narbonne known as Afrany (Barceló 1978: 24), and a fairly definitive form of Catalan had evolved by the eleventh century. Unlike most Romance languages, literary Catalan developed in prose rather than poetic form. Reflecting its political ties, elite culture in Catalonia had come under the influence of Provence, and courtly poetry produced by Catalans was written in Provençal until the fifteenth century (Sanchis Guarner 1980: 149, Veny 1986: 18). The earliest surviving texts in Catalan date to the twelfth century and are all administrative and religious: the compilation of Visigothic law called the Forum Judicum; the Homilies d'Organyà, a collection of sermons; and the legal code of the Usatges, a compilation of feudal custom and practice. By the thirteenth century, almost all official records of the Catalan governing body (Generalitat) and the town councils were kept in Catalan, and in 1276, the ruler Jaume I ordered that all documentation of the kingdom of Valencia (part of the Catalan territories) be kept in the vernacular rather than in Latin (Sanchis Guarner 1980: 162).

In the medieval period, Catalan was one of the most unified of the Romance languages in both grammar and orthography (Azevedo 1984). When the fortunes of Barcelona diminished in the fifteenth century, a Catalan literature continued to flourish in the new economic center of Valencia. Among the Catalan texts produced there was *Tirant Lo Blanc*, one of the most widely read secular works of fifteenth-century Europe (ibid.). Calling it "the best book of its kind in the world," Cervantes chose this to be the only book of chivalry saved from the burning of Quixote's library.

These brief notes give an indication of the developmental independence of Catalan, as well as a glimpse of the prestige that it once claimed, prestige that serves as a charter for the Catalan cultural movement. For a short description of the structure of Catalan, especially as it contrasts to that of Castilian, the interested reader may turn to Appendix A.

The Emergence of Catalonia

Like most of the Iberian peninsula, the area that would become Catalonia came under Visigothic and then Arab rule after the fall of the Roman Empire. By 801 A.D., after only 70 to 80 years of Moslem domination, Barcelona and the territory north of it later known as

"Old Catalonia" had been "reconquered" by the Franks (Salrach 1978: 25). The territory was loosely organized into the Carolingian feudal counties of the Hispanic March, an important buffer zone in the progressive reconquest of the peninsula. The boundary of Old Catalonia remained stable for 300 years, giving rise to differentiation not only from what would become Castile, but also from later-recovered territories such as Tarragona and Lleida that would form New Catalonia.

Catalonia began to develop as an independent entity in the ninth and tenth centuries with the foundation of a dynasty of indigenous Catalan counts who held at once Barcelona and a number of other counties. Although in theory Catalan counts continued to owe fealty to the Frankish monarch, the last Catalan count to be named by a French king was Guifré el Pilós in 878, and his descendants ruled in an unbroken line until 1410. Legend holds that the Catalan flag was created when the monarch dipped his fingers in the blood of the wounded Guifré and drew them across his shield, creating four red bars on a field of gold. (This "birth" of Catalonia in 878 was depicted in a comic book distributed in the campaign of 1979 by the Catalan Socialist Party to explain why Catalonia considers itself a nation.)

Over time, the Catalan counts ceased to honor their feudal duties to the king, and Bonnassie (1978: 39) holds that by the end of the eleventh century a Catalan state can be said to have emerged, built on an indigenous but quintessentially feudal base, codified under Ramon Berenguer I in the Usatges de Barcelona. The major differences between Catalonia and Castile are often traced to Catalonia's history as a feudal state, whereas feudalism never developed strongly in the rest of the peninsula. However, Vilar (1979a) argues that this difference was quantitative rather than qualitative, and that Catalonia was not a true feudal state itself (if the prototypical feudal state indeed ever existed; cf. Bloch 1961), since large feudal estates never consolidated in the narrow valleys of Catalonia.

Early Catalan Ascendancy

Although the linguistic differentiation of Catalonia from Castile has been traced to as early as the Roman period, and Catalan "nationalism" sometimes to as early as the reconquest of Barcelona from the Moslems, the critical historical antecedents of Catalan identity and nationalism lie in the Catalan commercial empire of the twelfth through fourteenth centuries. This period saw the expansion and consolidation of that empire, though not under an identifiable name. In 1137, the Catalan confederation of counties was united politically with the Crown of Aragon through the betrothal of the Count of Barcelona to the heiress of the Aragonese throne, and their offspring became "King of Aragon and Count of Barcelona." The name of Catalonia never appeared in royal titles, and that of Barcelona lost place over time, in what Soldevila considers the principal negative aspect of the union for Catalonia (cited in Sobrequés 1987: 21). (To add to the confusion, the twelfth-century compilers of the Usatges coined the term Principat, "Principality," to refer to Catalonia, a custom that continues today; ibid.) Nonetheless, in the twelfth century, the term Catalans became general to refer to the population of the various counties, and the name Catalonia appeared in official documents as early as 1178. The union under the Crown of Aragon was purely dynastic, and brought no erosion of the sovereignty of the two political entities. Catalonia and Aragon remained commercially, militarily, politically, and juridically distinct (ibid.: 14).

Under Jaume I, the "Conqueror" (1212–76), Valencia and the Balearics were conquered and came to be populated mostly by Catalans; today they are part of Catalan-speaking territory (known as Els Països Catalans, or the Catalan Countries), although not of Catalonia proper. Expansion and consolidation continued until around 1350, by which time the Catalano-Aragonese state was the largest in the Mediterranean and included Sicily, Sardinia, and even the dukedom of Athens in Greece.

The economic life of Catalonia benefited greatly from these political and military conquests; the salient differences between Catalonia and Spain arose from them; and the resulting accumulation of capital accorded Catalonia's economy security against political setbacks (Vilar 1979a: 153). Catalonia presided over one of the most extensive and powerful mercantile empires of the Mediterranean during this period. Although the region is not itself well endowed with natural resources, early industry sprang up in woolen textiles, and development spread throughout the Principality rather than remaining concentrated in one area.

Administrative advances kept pace with the commercial gains of medieval Catalonia, and modern Catalans point with pride to the early establishment of "democratic" political institutions. The twelfth-century Usatges, predating the English Magna Carta by a century, explicitly acknowledged legal equality between burghers (**ciutadans honrats**) and nobility (Giner 1984: 7). In the following century, a municipal council representing the estates of the urban population was organized in the form of the Council of One Hundred in Barcelona. Most significant to modern nationalists, by 1228 the first Catalan parliament (Corts) was constituted and empowered to present grievances as well as to advise on and consent to the financial undertakings of the Crown of Aragon. In 1359, the Generalitat, nominal ancestor of the contemporary governing body of Catalonia, first appeared, to administer the decisions of the Corts between their sessions.

Vilar (1979a) and Elliott (1963) both point out that too much has been made of the supposedly "democratic" character of these institutions. Most of the working population, attached to seigneurial dominions, had no representation whatsoever, and within the crown's cities, the oligarchies of the upper estates were in control of the deputies. The early "pactism" reflected in the Usatges, which is invoked as an essential characteristic of the Catalan nation, was in fact a pact between a limited urban ruling class and the king (Vilar 1979a: 171).

Nonetheless, Vilar gives credence to the nationalist school of history that has projected onto the fourteenth-century empire the national sentiment felt in the nineteenth century. Broadly democratic or not, the thirteenth-century Catalan Corts were the first representative body in Europe to have the characteristics of periodicity, legislative function, and fiscal control. And unlike that of England or France, the representative system was born not of agitation or revolution, but of spontaneous collaboration between the kings and their administrators, on the one hand, and the cities, the Church, and the Catalan nobility, on the other. Though Vilar contends that a national or group sentiment was a consequence rather than a cause of stable social structures, he nonetheless sees in thirteenth- and fourteenth-century Catalonia the most precocious nation-state of Europe: language, territory, economic life, political institutions, and cultural community were present at this early date (ibid.: 176–78). A premature bourgeois society, medieval Catalonia anticipated and even generated the major outline of world transformations toward industrial capitalism (Hansen 1977: 25).

Catalonia in Decline

In 1410, the Catalano-Aragonese dynasty found itself without an heir, and came to an end. By the Compromise of Caspe, Ferdinand I, the son of the king of Castile, was selected to take the throne, putting a non-Catalan ruler on the throne for the first time. This dynastic change is sometimes singled out by nationalists as the cause of the subsequent social, economic, and linguistic decline of Catalonia, but most historians view the relation as coincidental, attributing the steady social and economic decline in the fifteenth century to the eclipse of Mediterranean trade by transatlantic developments, and the linguistic decline to the corresponding growth in the influence of the Castilian court.

During the final decades of the fifteenth century, noble Catalan landowners clashed with the king over their "evil uses," or feudal privileges, which had been suspended by the crown. Vilar characterizes this not as the revolt of a nation against its sovereign, but as the political struggle of classes, and an attempt by landowners to shift the burden of a deepening agricultural and economic crisis onto their vassals (1979a: 228). Beginning with the marriage of Ferdinand (Ferran II) and Isabella in the late fifteenth century, Catalonia shared a common monarch with Castile. Catalan political individuality persisted for another century and a half, but economically, Catalonia's Mediterranean trade was clearly eclipsed by Castilian development in the Atlantic and the Americas. As Castile's power grew over the centuries, so Catalonia's fortunes continued to decline.

In 1640, the rural masses of Catalonia broke out in revolt against Castilian troops billeted there during the war against France; this became known as the Revolt of the Reapers (Els Segadors). The revolt was taken up by the urban elites, and the struggle was often phrased in national terms, as one of Catalonia against the centralizing pretensions of the Castilian monarchy (García Cárcel 1987). Though historians do not agree on the state of the economy and society during this period, and therefore on the cause of this revolt, Vilar holds that the Catalan economy was on the rise despite social instability. He therefore characterizes this revolt as the political reaction of a prosperous region against a decadent Castilian Empire (1979a: 324).

Catalonia seceded and placed itself under the protection of the crown of France, only to lose its territories north of the Pyrenees in the treaty negotiated between Castile and France in 1659. This war is invoked by modern nationalists as one of the major historical precedents for their movement; the unofficial national anthem of Catalonia, *Els Segadors*, refers to this war. The Revolt of the Reapers was the first time "the land" and historical charter were invoked as the ideological justification of the defense not only of the liberties but of the nation of Catalonia (Vilar 1979a: 327).

By 1705, Catalonia once again found itself at war with Castile, this time in the war of the Spanish Succession. In the final instance this was an attempt on the part of the Catalan urban bourgeoisie to reestablish a Spain oriented toward the Mediterranean, rather than an attempt to secede from foreign domination. They sought a decentralized structure that would be the "liberation of all Spain"; even in its most definitive moment, the Catalan position was phrased as one of Spanish rather than Catalan nationalism (Vilar 1979a: 358–60).

Once again, however, Catalonia placed its faith in the wrong party, supporting the Hapsburg Archduke Charles against Castile's choice, the Bourbon Philip of Anjou. When the Hapsburg became Charles VI of the Holy Roman Empire in 1711, he abandoned Catalonia to Castile in the bargain. Catalonia continued to resist until September 11, 1714, when Barcelona was taken. This date is conventionally singled out as the end of Catalonia as a discrete political entity, and it is commemorated, ironically, as the national holiday of Catalonia. In 1716 the decree of the Nova Planta (New Foundation) abolished the Catalan Corts, the Generalitat, the Council of One Hundred, and the local fiscal and monetary system—in short, all the independent institutions of the Catalan government, as well as independent cultural institutions such as the universities (Martínez Shaw 1978: 53).

In spite of the political losses, the years 1730 to 1790 brought demographic growth to Catalonia, as well as economic strength through the expansion of Catalan textile commerce in the colonial markets across the Atlantic. During the era of Carlos III, there appear to have been few conflicts of interest between the Spanish state and the Catalan region, and Catalans did not invoke local sentiment for either political or linguistic autonomy (Vilar 1979a: 71). Bourgeois prosperity and the congruence of the economic aspirations of Catalonia and Castile led Catalans to identity their interests with Castile during the eighteenth century.

With the Spanish market open to them, Catalans began to monopolize the cotton trade and transport within the peninsula. Growth of agriculture led to the creation of a new rural-urban bourgeoisie, based on the distinctive Catalan **pubilla-hereu** impartible-inheritance system for immovable property. Rural landowners' movable property went to stake their second sons to business, trade, or industry in the city, and this contributed to the expansion of the cotton industry (Hansen 1977). Although the Bourbon monarchy's program of political unification of Spain separated the Catalan ruling classes from the sources of power, its economic programs such as encouragement of industry, state-subsidized construction of highways, etc., all fell in very well with the ambitions of the new Catalan bourgeoisie (Solé-Tura 1974: 23, Martínez Shaw 1978). Vilar (1979b: 97) takes the Catalan bourgeoisie's abandonment of Catalan for Castilian in high cultural activities as a sign that it had never felt itself to be more Spanish than at the end of the eighteenth century. But it has also been said that it was Catalonia that virtually colonized Spain in economic and industrial terms (Vicens Vives 1958, cited in Solé-Tura 1974: 24), a hyperbole that nonetheless points up the source of later tension.

The Decline of the Catalan Language

With the decline of Catalan fortunes and the rise in importance of the Castilian court in the fifteenth century, the Catalan language began to decline correspondingly in prestige. Castilian appeared in formal domains of use, in a diglossic relation to Catalan (in Fishman's [1967] sense of diglossia as a functional compartmentalization of codes, regardless of their linguistic relation), and language shift began to take effect in some sectors. In 1561, the Spanish Inquisition made the use of Castilian obligatory in its trials (Nadal 1987: 27). But until the eighteenth century, Catalan monolingualism predominated within Catalan territory, and the use of Castilian was clearly that of a foreign language, according to Azevedo (1984).

Catalan tradition points to the Nova Planta as the death knell of the Catalan language, or at least of its use in official and formal domains. The decree itself (Article 5) mandated that Castilian be used in appeals court (Audiencia) cases. A much-quoted secret royal instruction in 1716 enjoined regional administrators to do everything possible to introduce Castilian "all around in a subtle way" that would not alert the population to the efforts. But the decline of Catalan was based as much on social and economic factors as on official policy; 1716 only brought official sanction to the ongoing process. With the emigration to the Castilian court, the Catalan aristocracy had begun to become castilianized in the late fifteenth century (Nadal 1987: 28). By the seventeenth century, there is evidence that this language shift on the part of the dominant class had consequences for the general population, making familiarity with Castilian a possibility if not an everyday occurrence (ibid.).

Official efforts to supplant Catalan were made throughout the eighteenth century; for example, in 1768–71, Carlos III issued decrees ordering that all primary and secondary schooling be conducted in Castilian, and in 1772, a royal decree ordered commercial establishments to keep books in Castilian (Ardit, Balcells, and Sales 1980: 39). However, the reach of these decrees was limited. Ardit, Balcells, and Sales contend that language use in schools depended less on the will of Madrid than on the attitude of each bishop, religious order, and town council responsible for education. While the Jesuits had been a strong castilianizing force since the sixteenth century, the Mallorcan Franciscans continued to publish and teach in Catalan (ibid.: 43–44).

The leading Catalan intellectuals of the eighteenth century did use Castilian for their work; most were alumni of Jesuit schools. But their literary, judicial, and archival works do not represent all the domains of writing. Major commercial houses kept their books in Catalan, the military orders and most of the guilds kept all records in Catalan (Ardit, Balcells, and Sales 1980: 41–45), and many nobles and bourgeois elites carried out their correspondence in Catalan (McDonogh 1981, Vilar 1979a). The most important point here is that literary decadence should not be confused with linguistic decadence. Though there was an irrefutable institution of diglossia, or shift to Castilian in formal domains, this says nothing about oral and informal uses. In a period when a large portion of the population was illiterate (Ardit, Balcells, and Sales 1980: 41), it would be grossly misleading to characterize the status of the language by its literary uses alone.

Nineteenth-Century Catalan Nationalism

The eighteenth-century unity of purpose between Madrid and Catalonia dissolved in the nineteenth century as the structural differences between a more industrialized and bourgeois Catalonia and a still essentially agrarian Spain became aggravated. The contradiction between the agrarian interests of the oligarchy of Castile, with their consolidated latifundia, and the Catalan need for protectionism and retention of colonial markets became the central issue of the nineteenth century.

The story of nineteenth-century Catalan nationalism has most often been understood as the story of the frustrated attempt at bourgeois revolution by an industrial elite (Hansen 1977). Vilar summarizes the state of affairs late in the century: "The development of capitalism . . . is, in its essence, a development of inequality. A relation between a colony and a metropolis had installed itself in Spain between the country as a whole and its industrialized region, with all the rancors that this presumes. But here the colonized are the majority. And they have the State! This cannot go on. It is the source of the wound" (Vilar 1979a: 66; my translation).

The rallying cry of Catalan political leaders was "National Industry!" Throughout most of the nineteenth-century struggles, however, by "national" the Catalans meant Spain. National market, national industry, national production always referred to the Spanish nation (Solé-Tura 1974: 57). Political appeals were phrased as appeals to Spanish interests: *"España con industria, rica y fuerte"* (Spain with industry, rich and strong) (Hansen 1977). Vilar, however, points out that national industry was in fact Catalan industry. For example, 90 percent of the cotton-textile industry was concentrated in Catalonia (1979a: 62).

From 1885 to 1917, "A class aspired to control a state," writes Vilar (1979a: 55), and it was only after seeing itself denied control of the Spanish state that the Catalan leadership fell back on demands for regional political autonomy. The Catalan industrial bourgeoisie was unable either to gain control of the instrument of the state or to identify its interests as those of Spain as a whole; only then did Catalonia become the "nation" and Spain "the state" (although Riquer 1987b: 19 questions this dominant interpretation, and claims that the Catalan bourgeoisie had lost the leading role in the construction of Spanish liberalism as early as 1843). It was the loss in 1898 of the last American colonial market monopoly, Cuba and Puerto Rico, that finally led the Catalan bourgeoisie to express its interests in Catalan nationalist terms. Political regionalism was united to the earlier cultural regionalism that had brought about the literary and cultural revival known as the Renaixença, and the concept of a distinctive Catalan nation grew.

Linguistic Revival and the Growth of Nationalism

Official linguistic policy in the nineteenth century had continued that of the eighteenth century. In 1858, the Law of Public Instruction confirmed the Decree of 1780, mandating the use of Castilian in primary and secondary schools. In 1862, the Law of Notaries ordered that all legal documentation be set out in Castilian. In 1867, a royal order prohibited plays that were "exclusively written in any of the dialects of the provinces of Spain," although the order was annulled the following year (Ardit, Balcells, and Sales 1980: 253). But as was pointed out above for the eighteenth century, it is incorrect to say, as do Inglehart and Woodward (1972: 371, citing Brenan 1962), that "in 1860 [Catalan] was spoken only in the most remote and obscure villages." It is true that at the time of the Renaixença the near-complete literary demise had left Catalan standard grammar and orthography in a chaotic state (Azevedo 1984). But literary revival is not linguistic revival; Catalan was still the habitual language of the urban and rural masses as well as the rural aristocracy (McDonogh 1981).

The Catalan cultural renaissance, inspired by Romantic philosophy and fueled by the economic boom of the industrial revolution, began in the domain of literature. The Renaixença is conventionally dated to 1833, with Carles Aribau's nostalgic poem, *Oda a la Pàtria* (Ode to the Homeland). Shortly thereafter, in 1841, the first general periodical in Catalan was founded. The Floral Games, harking back to the poetry contests of the medieval period in Provence and Catalonia, were revived in 1859, and the first Catalan daily, *El Diari Català*, appeared in 1879.

Two seminal but divergent statements of Catalanism arose from the economic, political, and intellectual ferment: Almirall's *Lo catalanisme* in 1886, and Torras i Bages's *La tradició catalana* in 1892. Almirall envisioned a modern bourgeois Catalonia with a personality defined not by tradition but by urban and industrial progress (Solé-Tura 1974: 108). His principal aim was to defend urban capitalism against a stifling centralist bureaucracy. The bishop Torras i Bages, on the other hand, enshrined the Catholic conservatism of the Catalan countryside. He exalted rural life, the land, religion, the family, and language. Land and language took on a mystical significance, and the Catalan stem family was seen as chartered by divine inspiration (ibid.: 81).

These apparently contradictory themes of Catalanist ideology were brought together after the turn of the century by Enric Prat de la Riba in the definitive statement of bourgeois Catalanism, *La nacionalitat catalana*, moving it from the realm of regionalism to nationalism. The contradictions between the two distinct visions of society were not resolved, and Solé-Tura, among others, sees them as leading to the eventual undoing of bourgeois Catalanism. Nonetheless, the two ideological visions remain powerful. For example, in the 1980 election-campaign literature, the nationalist candidate Jordi Pujol (a banker) invoked both his rural roots and his entrepreneurial élan; Pujol became president of Catalonia.

The turn of the century saw the continued growth of the linguistic movement. The year 1906 brought the First International Congress of the Catalan Language, and the Institute of Catalan Studies was founded in Barcelona in 1907. In the period 1913–32, the lexicographer and grammarian Pompeu Fabra consolidated a Catalan literary standard for the first time in centuries, in works that still hold considerable authority today.

As Benet (1978) documents, Castilianist ideologues have ridiculed the literary revival of Catalan as artificial, the resuscitation of a dead language. Vilar (1979a: 76) points out the weakness of this criticism; the more artificial the task, the more remarkable its success, especially in a period of high literary achievement for Castilian (the Generation of '98). And Vilar leaves little doubt about its success. In his portrait of early-twentieth-century Barcelona, painted from personal experience, Catalan is a language very alive at all levels—high culture and literature, the daily press, and the popular vernacular. Vilar contrasts this "hardly banal spectacle" with Provence, which experienced a similar literary movement but nothing like the popular success of the Catalan movement. Vilar's analysis of the reasons for this success, however, is clear: "It is here that we note the relative order of political and linguistic reality. It is without a doubt because they speak Catalan that the Catalans have been able to preserve a group consciousness. But it is above all when they have felt this group consciousness with the most force that they have refused to forget Catalan. . . . Historically, it is the *growth* of linguistic differentiation that is striking; it *follows*, rather than precedes, the progress of regional demands" (Vilar 1979a: 75; my translation, emphasis in original).

Twentieth-Century Contradictions

The industrial strength that was the base of Catalanism's successes was also the seed of its destruction. The revolution of September 1868 in Spain brought six years of agitated politics that led the Catalan bourgeoisie to support the restoration of a strong central state after the fall of the First Republic in 1874, to eradicate the "subversive and dangerous" elements of syndicalism (Riquer 1987: 40–41). Failing to rationalize their small family-based industries, the factory owners grew increasingly harsh and repressive toward the workers, turning to the central government to suppress strikes and protect the factories (Giner 1984: 24–25). During the same period, the most active sectors of the working class, unable to negotiate with employers or the state, became increasingly radicalized and anarchosyndicalist.

The first political party of conservative Catalan nationalism, the Lliga Regionalista (Regionalist League) was founded in 1901. In the Spanish elections of 1907, this party organized a coalition called Solidaritat Catalana, which swept the elections. Political Catalanism appeared to be in a position to achieve its aims, but the proletarian uprisings of the Tragic Week of 1909 brought to a head the class conflicts that had been growing throughout the last decades (Ullman 1968). As the Lliga called for—and got—the execution of the alleged Anarchist leaders of the revolt, the class contradictions of Catalanism became patent.

In 1914 the Lliga, under the leadership of Prat de la Riba, succeeded in establishing the Mancomunitat of Catalonia, the first governing body of the Catalan provinces in two centuries. The Manco-munitat lasted only until 1925, and its powers were limited, uniting only those already pertaining to the provincial administration. Main areas of advance were in language and education, and the principal power of the Mancomunitat was its ability to borrow money to finance Catalanist projects.

In addition to the Anarchists, a counterpoint to the force of the Lliga was the Radical party of Alexander Lerroux, an Andalusian. Beginning in the 1920's, working-class immigration from the south of Spain had taken on significant proportions. Lerroux's incendiary rhetoric was both anticlerical and anti-Catalan; the "Young Barbarians," as his followers were known, were incited to riot against the Church and Catalan industrialists alike. Lerroux's ideas and motivations are still somewhat mysterious, but he continued to play a political role through the period of the Second Republic. Though members of the Lliga claimed, and popular lore still holds, that Lerroux was in the pay of the central government to disrupt Catalonia, the facts are not clear. This somewhat bizarre historical figure is a strong presence in the memory of modern Catalans. His name is still commonly invoked today in the term **lerrouxisme** to discredit any political activity that appears to pit the immigrant workers of Catalonia against Catalan nationalism. The implication of conspiracy with the central government that this accusation carries is still a powerful deterrent to rhetoric that addresses principally the immigrant working class.

The Lliga's pretensions to Catalanism were abandoned definitively in 1923, when it welcomed the Spanish dictatorship of Primo de Rivera. The dictatorship met conservative industrialists' desire to control the working class, but also cut into Catalan privileges, disbanded the Mancomunitat, and suppressed the Catalan language again. The Catalan industrial bourgeoisie never succeeded in its bid to become a ruling class, because of its failure to resolve its internal conflicts with the workers.

The Second Spanish Republic and the War Years

A liberal Catalanism emerged in the nationalist Esquerra Republicana (Republican Left), led by radicalized sectors of the lower bourgeoisie. Although its Catalanist sentiment was strong, the party's resolution of the conflict between Catalanism and class organization was unclear. The avowed aim of its leader, Francesc Macià, was "a small house and a vegetable garden" for every citizen. The party demonstrated its wide appeal with sweeping victories in the 1931 Spanish elections and the 1932 elections for the Catalan Parlament. Under the Second Spanish Republic (1931–39), Catalonia was granted a Statute of Autonomy (1932), and the Esquerra proved to be the leading political force within this framework.

Though the power of the new Catalan government was restricted, the Statute gave substantial home control over administration, education, and services, and these were quickly catalanized. Within two weeks of the coming of the Republic in April 1931, all dictates against the use of Catalan in primary schools that had been issued since 1923 were abolished. The plebiscite on the Statute of Autonomy approved Catalan as the official language of Catalonia. This was later modified to co-officiality with Castilian by the Spanish parliament. Nonetheless, Catalan became the public and official language of the Catalan Parlament and Generalitat, and of the majority of schools and media (Guardiola 1980: 17).

A fragile truce held between the workers and liberal nationalists in this period, and Vilar explains that this derived from common experiences under the Primo de Rivera dictatorship ushered in by the Lliga: "Unity was born from the demands of the opposition. . . . The same enemies, the same memories, fed the rancor of the workers' groups and the Catalanist groups. Civil guards, police, soldiers—almost always Castilians—embodied, in the Catalonia of 1928, at the same time national oppression and social oppression" (Vilar 1979a: 47; my translation).

Thus the anarchosyndicalist ideology of the increasingly non-Catalan, Castilian-speaking proletariat fell into line with the more liberal native movement for autonomy. Contradictions between the two were temporarily suspended in favor of the common cause of opposing the dictatorship (we will see this process repeated as we explore more recent Catalan politics). The truce was at best an uneasy one. Lluís Companys, founding member of Esquerra and later President of the Catalan Generalitat, was a labor lawyer who had defended the anarchist CNT (Confederación Nacional de Trabajo), but Giner claims that once in power, Esquerra leaders harassed Anarchists (1984: 33). It became increasingly clear that proletarian and

Catalan nationalist interests were not identical. Nonetheless, as the complicated Spanish political life became more and more polarized, Catalonia came to be viewed as the "bulwark of the Republic against the onslaught of the right" (Jones 1984: 100).

Civil war came in 1936, fueled partially by centralist resentment of developments in the minority peripheries, but the result largely of the continuing struggle between an old order of society and a new one, and of the internecine warfare within the Left. These struggles, the short-lived attempt to establish a revolutionary society in Barcelona, and the stolid anti-Fascist stance of Catalonia, as well as the tragic outcome of the Civil War, are well documented in scholarly and popular literature and will not be reviewed here (cf. Orwell 1952, Brenan 1962, Jackson 1965, Kern 1978).

The Postwar Period: Political and Linguistic Repression

The aftermath of the war brought the disbanding of Catalonia as an autonomous region and a return to its administration as four separate provinces. Enacting the belief that "Spain is a thing made by Castile" (Ortega y Gasset 1936, cited in Benet 1978: 70), in the early postwar period, the Franco government took severe repressive measures against the Catalan language and culture as well as against the revolutionary proletariat. All public uses of Catalan were quickly abolished, and an attempt was made to reduce the language to dialect status in the consciousness of its speakers. Benet (1978) documents the prohibition of Catalan in publications, government offices, schools, posters, street signs, shop signs, and advertising. The penalties were fines and loss of position for individuals, and the closing of schools and institutions. Others have reported that in many situations, even informal oral use of Catalan was considered illegal or dangerous; *Habla en cristiano* (Speak Christian) and *No ladres; habla la lengua del imperio* (Don't bark; speak the language of the empire) are said to have been common refrains. The following quote from a Fascist textbook of the period exemplifies the Francoist attempts at dialectalization:

(Q.) Are there any languages spoken in Spain besides the Castilian language?

(A.) It may be said that in Spain only the Castilian language is spoken, for besides it, only Basque is spoken, which is used as the only language in a few Basque hamlets alone; it is reduced to the functions of a dialect because of its linguistic and philological poverty.

(Q.) And what are the main dialects spoken in Spain?

(A.) [They] are four: Catalan, Valencian, Mallorcan, and Galician.

(*Catecismo Patriótico Español*, cited in Azevedo, 1984)

Because of the institutionalization of diglossia, today there are virtually no monolingual adult speakers of Catalan, and a high proportion of Catalan speakers do not read or write their native language. Nonetheless, for the most part Catalans maintained a tenacious loyalty to their language. Catalan was never displaced from informal communication between native speakers of most social strata, and its use in public was a significant aspect of the leftist and nationalist political protests that arose in the later postwar period.

With legitimate political outlets closed to them, the Catalan people turned to diverse forms of voluntary organizations—already a traditional vehicle—as a forum in which to express the Catalan spirit. Religious pilgrimages to the holy mountain Montserrat, mountaineering clubs, scout troops, and art and music circles became particularly important, as did the folkdance the **sardana** when it was again permitted. In the late 1950's, a language movement began to spring up again, as Franco loosened his grip on Spain and made some moves to liberalize the dictatorship.

From 1959 to 1969, various petitions were submitted, first by intellectuals and then by large numbers of organizations, in favor of the "normalization" of the Catalan language. In the mid-1950's, a religious magazine in Catalan began publication. And in the early 1960's, a private foundation began offering language courses and training a small number of teachers. In 1967, a Department of Catalan Language was even permitted at the University of Barcelona. Throughout this period, there was a strong popular movement toward quasi-legal public uses of the language, especially in music. Heroes of the Nova Cançó (New Music) followed the model of American folk-protest music, recording and performing in Catalan (when permitted) to the popular acclaim of a large public. Finally, a new education law in 1970 authorized the teaching of (but not in) Catalan in schools, although the implementation of this was impeded until 1975, the year of Franco's death.

The Postwar Period: An Immigration Explosion

At the same time that Catalonia was struggling with Francoist repression, it was undergoing radical social change. Working-class immigration from the impoverished agrarian south of Spain had already been an important factor in the prewar years, and Barcelona was the primary destination of this immigration. But it is generally claimed that these earlier immigrants, moving into working-class Catalan neighborhoods, integrated themselves into the fabric of Catalan life and assimilated to the Catalan language. Few data exist to confirm this assimilation, and there is some reason to believe that ethnic conflicts entered into the divisions between the working class and liberals in the prewar and Civil War periods. It is nevertheless the case that today there are many older immigrants who speak Catalan, and many Castilian-surnamed descendants who are linguistically and ethnically Catalan.

Postwar immigration, however, met a different fate. After recovery from the immediate, devastating aftereffects of the war, the wave of immigration from the south resumed and grew to massive proportions. Clearinghouses and barracks had to be set up to handle the flow; at times, trains loaded with immigrants were turned back. Between 1950 and 1975, nearly 1.4 million immigrants entered Catalonia; the vast majority of these ended up in the Barcelona metropolitan area. This flood compares to a natural growth during the same period of only a little over 1 million (Recolons et al. 1979).

Escaping from the grinding poverty afflicting the southern rural proletariat, immigrants were most often uneducated and unskilled. Linz (1975: 395) points out that Catalonia probably attracted a larger share of illiterate immigrants from the poorest regions of Spain than did the Basque country, another migrant destination. Many entered the construction industry as day laborers, but the chemical industry was also growing, replacing textiles in importance in many areas. As unskilled laborers were brought in to fill the lowest rungs of the occupational ladder, the autochthonous labor force moved up into skilled and managerial positions. The socioeconomic difference between native Catalans and immigrants, who are almost all of Castilian-speaking origin, is striking. In spite of the presence of a Castilian political and administrative elite placed in Catalonia by the Franco government, native Catalans are heavily concentrated in the

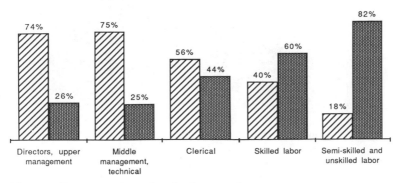

Fig. 2.1. Representation of native-born and immigrants in Catalan industry. Source: Sáez 1980: 32.

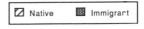

highest occupations, and immigrants are concentrated in the lowest levels of manual labor (see Fig. 2.1). Education levels and the distribution of children in public and private schools reported in Figures 2.2–2.4 are additional reflections of this social inequality. Though these patterns may be due primarily to the low levels of education and occupational training among immigrant forces, rather than to overt discrimination, they generate potentially long-term consequences (Maluquer Sostres 1963, 1966).

Because of the rapid rate of immigration, the sheer numbers involved, and the lack of urban planning under Franco, this second wave of immigration was forced into crowded, high-rise living in slapdash new dormitory suburbs. The Barcelona metropolitan area contains almost 67 percent of the total 5.66 million inhabitants of Catalonia. All of Barcelona is quintessentially urban, in both the good and the bad sense. But in these suburbs, the polluted atmosphere is unrelieved by greenery or the graceful architecture for which Barcelona is famous. Infrastructural services are minimal, and children play in dusty, unpaved plazas between row after row of grimy cement-block apartment structures. Not many Catalan speakers are found in these worker suburbs; and those who do live there are usually found in the core of the older village or city around which the new developments grew.

This phenomenon creates a separate reality in Catalonia. With the onset of economic stagnation and finally crisis in the 1970's, im-

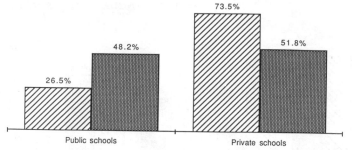

73.5%

48.2%

51.8%

26.5%

Public schools   Private schools

Fig. 2.2. Representation of Catalan- and Castilian-speaking students in public and private elementary schools, Barcelona city, 1976. Source: Arnau 1980: 102.

LANGUAGE
Catalan   Castilian

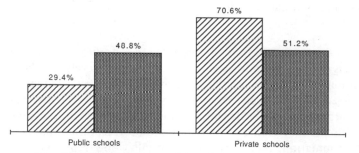

70.6%

48.8%

51.2%

29.4%

Public schools   Private schools

Fig. 2.3. Distribution of Catalan- and Castilian-speaking teachers in public and private elementary schools, Barcelona province, 1978. Source: Arnau 1980: 111.

LANGUAGE
Catalan   Castilian

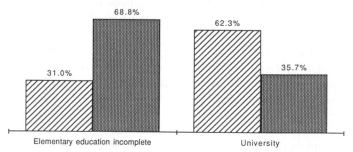

68.8%

62.3%

31.0%

35.7%

Elementary education incomplete   University

Fig. 2.4. Representation of Catalan and Castilian speakers at two levels of educational attainment, Barcelona province (excluding capital), 1975. Source: Reixach 1985: 138–39.

LANGUAGE
Catalan   Castilian

migration tapered off, but its impact is still massive. In 1970, 40 percent of the population of Catalonia was non-native-born (Sáez 1980). Of those born in Catalonia, a high percentage are in fact children of Castilian-speaking immigrants, who have a higher fertility rate than autochthonous Catalans, for reasons of both age and class/cultural norms (Pinilla de las Heras 1979).

Thus, one of the greatest fears that small European countries might harbor about their "guest workers"—that they will numerically overwhelm the native population—has virtually come to pass in Catalonia. It is particularly critical that this has occurred in a region with a strong sense of nationhood but none of the institutional mechanisms for protecting its identity. The situation is made more complicated by the fact that these immigrant workers are speakers of dialects of the official state language, Castilian, and usually consider themselves Spaniards (*españoles*). In all of Catalonia, it was estimated at the time of this study, only about 52 percent of the adult population spoke Catalan as the home or habitual language (Junyent 1979). Analyses based on the 1975 census update reveal that this figure falls as low as 22 percent in the areas surrounding the city of Barcelona (*Avui* 1982; Termes 1983). These data reflect actual demographic change more than linguistic shift on the part of Catalans. Given the differences in fertility rates between Catalans and immigrants, it is not surprising that in the province of Barcelona only about 37 percent of primary school children are native speakers of Catalan (Arnau 1980).

It is ironic that the same factor has created both the strengths and the weaknesses of the Catalan nationalist position. Relatively early economic development gave Catalonia the material resources to maintain a strong sense of identity and the power to adopt an independent stance toward the central government (Medina 1975). But it has also led to the undermining of the ethnic homogeneity of the region, the implantation of the Castilian language at the vernacular level, and the accentuation of class divisions in attempts at political mobilization.

With the death of Franco in 1975, political possibilities opened up again in Spain, particularly for the culturally distinct regions, and changes in the fragile new democracy began to be negotiated. In the first elections of the post-Franco period, the euphoria was a shared one. As in Vilar's Barcelona of the 1920's, common rancors and common memories of oppression under the Franco dictatorship brought the working class and Catalan nationalism together; "this much Catalonia owes the general" (Giner 1984: 34; cf. Clark 1980). One million people are estimated to have turned out in Barcelona to wave the Catalan flag in the 1977 celebration of the Catalan national holiday. In the first elections, a leftist coalition called the Entesa dels Catalanas swept the Senate polls much as Solidaritat Catalana had in 1906. But once the symbolic question of Catalonia's existence had been so resoundingly answered, the real questions behind it—what kind of Catalonia, who rules, what language do they speak—became the focus of attention. The sociolinguistic and ethnic facets of these questions are addressed in the remainder of this book.

CHAPTER THREE |||| A CRISIS IN THE
                      CONCEPT OF
                      IDENTITY

In the fall of 1977, Josep Tarradellas, a minister of the Generalitat
under the Second Republic and president in exile during the Franco
years, returned from France to preside over the newly reinstated, provisional Catalan government. Arriving in Barcelona, his salute to the
people was, "Citizens of Catalonia, I am here" (**Ciutadans de Catalunya, ja sóc aquí**).* Tarradellas's use of "citizens," instead of the
more usual "Catalans," distressed some of his audience (Argente et
al. 1979). Yet the president reported in news interviews that he had
given much thought to the formulation of his greeting, searching for
a way to avoid the potentially divisive and exclusive term "Catalans"
(*Grama* 1979).

Two years after Tarradellas's return, Barcelona prepared for another important step in what was called the "national reconstruction" of Catalonia. The months of September and October 1979
brought a campaign for a referendum on the Statute of Autonomy.
Only a simple majority of the votes cast was needed to enact the Stat-

---

*What Tarradellas actually said was, "Citizens of Catalonia, I am here to work"
(**Ciutadans de Catalunya, ja sóc aquí per a treballar**). However, only the first part of
his statement has been preserved in political folklore. So well known is the phrase that
it is sometimes used by people as a joking entrance line when joining a gathering.

ute, but Catalonia's political leaders felt that a high abstention rate would be a moral defeat. Parties from almost the entire political spectrum, excluding only the extreme Right and splintered groups of the far Left, joined the provisional government in urging support of the Statute. Two key slogans echoed throughout the campaign: "Now more than ever, one single people" (**Ara més que mai, un sol poble**), and "All those who live and work in Catalonia are Catalan" (**És català tothom qui viu i treballa a Catalunya**).*

Both the president's circumlocution and the insistent campaign messages pointed to what had become an acute issue in Catalonia: the problem of defining and symbolizing group identity, given the major changes wrought by massive immigration in the twentieth century. The political slogans suggested that there was only one politically relevant ethnic identity in Catalonia, but by their very existence and insistence they betrayed the fact that there was more than one. As Geertz has said of the "new states," nationalist slogans are a hope, not a description (1973: 315). The political appeals of the referendum campaign were self-conscious attempts to surmount linguistic and ethnic boundaries that had migrated into Catalonia. By declaring everyone to be Catalan, politicians set the terms of discourse on the nationalist issue. Those who wished to repudiate a pro-Catalan position had to take offensive (in both senses) action. This political strategy had one shortcoming, however: a declaration of identity does not automatically make new members susceptible to the emotional power of such ethnic symbols as the language.

As Simmel wrote, "The first condition of having to deal with somebody at all is to know with whom one has to deal" (1950: 307). Defining Catalan identity had become a cottage industry in the Barcelona of 1979 and 1980. Hardly a day passed that one could not open a newspaper and find an editorial commentary, several letters to the editor, and/or the announcement of a public conference addressing the question of "who is Catalan." Spain's leading weekly newsmagazine represented the identity problem in Catalonia with its cover illustration of a puzzled-looking man wrapped in the Catalan flag and wearing an Andalusian hat (*Cambio 16*, 1979). The title,

---

*This definition of Catalan identity was actually formulated in the 1960's by Jordi Pujol in his underground, clandestinely distributed papers. In the 1980 elections Pujol, a conservative nationalist, became president of Catalonia. His rhetorical formula, however, was also used in the campaigns by other parties and their candidates.

"Cataluces or Andalanes?" (based on wordplay with the Castilian terms *catalanes* and *andaluces*), pointed up the most critical aspect of the identity problem: dichotomization. In spite of ambiguous terminologies and ambivalent sentiments, the question of ethnicity in Catalonia returned again and again to choice and confrontation between two contrasting identities.

This chapter considers the definitions and significance of alternative identities in the Barcelona of 1979–80. Understandings of ethnic identity offered by informants in interviews and informal discussions, as well as those culled from newspapers, books, and public meetings, form the basis for this analysis. I treat these different understandings systematically and somewhat abstractly, rather than letting them speak for themselves, but my purpose is not to eliminate contradictions among them in order to arrive at a single cultural model of ethnic identity. Rather, by ordering as far as possible the welter of spontaneous and strategic commentary on the issue, I hope not to gloss over but to reveal the conflictive and contested.*

Who is Catalan?

The answer to this question is partly legal, partly popular. The legal definition of "Catalan" was developed for the Statute of Autonomy of 1932 and reinstated in the Statute of 1979 (Article 6). The "political condition of Catalan" is defined therein as pertaining to any Spanish citizen who has administrative residence in any municipality of Catalonia. This definition was called into question in the campaigns of 1979–80 only by political parties claiming to represent the interests of Andalusian and Aragonese immigrants (PSA: Socialist Party of Andalusia, and, for a brief time, Socialist Party of Aragon). Representatives of these parties demanded but did not win a clause in the Statute that would explicitly allow immigrants to retain the political status of their region of origin (*Mundo Diario* 1979).

Turning from legalistic to popular definitions of Catalan identity,

---

*Because this is an effort to generalize and abstract from informants' discourse, much of what follows in this chapter is written in a generic present tense. This conventional usage does not imply that the same generalizations hold for other historical moments; only the state of affairs at a particular critical juncture in Catalan history is represented here.

there are basically four alternate criteria: birthplace, descent, senti-ment/behavior, and language. Though each of these may be invoked and accepted in certain restricted contexts, it is the criterion of lan-guage that is both the most commonly used and the most powerful.

People may claim group membership according to a simple geo-graphical birthplace criterion. Thus a young mother reports, "My husband and I are Andalusian, but our children are Catalan." A letter to the editor of a daily newspaper begins, "I'm a Murcian, and I have two Catalan sons." Here, the label "Catalan" carries no cultural or linguistic connotations, and the contrasting labels always refer to other regions of Spain—Andalusian, Murcian, Castilian, Galician, etc.

This birthplace criterion is dominant in the immigrant-origin en-claves. When directly asked, "Who is Catalan?," teenaged Castilian-speaking children of immigrants almost unanimously used the birth-place criterion to identify themselves and their classmates as Cata-lans if they were born in the Barcelona area. In the informal discus-sions that followed, however, they shifted tacitly to other criteria of identity. In discussing their lives, these same teenagers would speak of themselves as "Castilian" (*castellano*) and contrast their behavior to that of Catalans, showing that the consciously claimed birthplace criterion had not been incorporated into the way that they made sense of their world. Moreover, autochthonous Catalans who are lin-guistically and culturally Catalan do not often concur, even in for-mal interviews, with second-generation immigrant claims to Catalan identity based on birthplace alone.

A second obvious possible criterion of identity is descent, and the children of those recognized as Catalan are indeed usually automat-ically identified as Catalan. However, the notion of "blood" or race has not been greatly elaborated in either popular or political Catalan tradition, in contrast to attitudes in the Basque region (Heiberg 1980, Shabad and Gunther 1982). Long descent lines are not usually nec-essary to qualify one as Catalan; rather they are used only to dem-onstrate the profundity of one's Catalan identity. Occasionally a person will be disqualified from being "really Catalan" by another because of a non-Catalan parent, but it is indicative of the permea-bility of ethnic boundaries in Catalonia that only rarely are references to Catalan grandparents made in order to claim full "membership."

Many very Catalanist informants proudly point to an immigrant grandparent who learned Catalan and was absorbed into the Catalan family, and Catalan nationalists with Castilian last names are numerous. Catalan leaders often cite Catalonia's tradition as a **terra de pas** (frontier zone) that has historically absorbed peoples and ideas from other lands, and are optimistic that this tradition has not ended.

A third criterion of Catalan identity, that of sentimental allegiance to Catalonia, is used in two very different ways. Some Catalan nationalists assert that it is necessary to demonstrate loyalty to the language, customs, and institutions of Catalonia in order to be Catalan, even if one is of Catalan descent for generations. This denies membership to the upper bourgeoisie who not only shifted to habitual use of Castilian in the late nineteenth and the twentieth centuries, but also oriented socially and politically to Madrid: "the Milans del Bosch come from a Catalan family; they were Catalans, but now they're not" (Termes 1983: 284). One commentator speaks of "renegade Catalans" who "in practice are not really Catalan" (Vinyals i Soler 1980a). Another writes that "it is not necessary to call the upper bourgeoisie Catalan, but rather that which it is and has always been, Spanish" (Sellares 1980).*

On the other hand, emotional loyalty may also be cited by first-generation immigrants as the most important criterion of Catalan identity. They may not have been born in Catalonia, or to Catalan parents, but some immigrants say they feel Catalan, identify with and love Catalonia, and thus may designate themselves as Catalan. They are supported in this belief by much of the political rhetoric: "He is Catalan who has freely chosen to accept a manner of being, a philosophy of life, a language, and other symbols" (Vinyals i Soler 1980b); "We admit as Catalans everyone who behaves like a Catalan. And this behavior obviously means dedication, enthusiasm, loyalty to that which is fundamental for Catalonia" (Cruells 1965: 15).

These three different criteria of identity, though accepted in certain contexts, are all completely eclipsed by a single predominant shibboleth of group membership: language. In common parlance, a Catalan is a person who uses Catalan in a native-like way as a first, home, and/or habitual language. Though this is not the definition

---

*McDonogh (1981, 1986a) gives a more precise and detailed account of cultural and linguistic change among this elite.

necessarily given when people are asked directly, it is one that emerges consistently in discussions about the social and political situation of Catalonia, of Barcelona, and of neighborhood and family.

Castilian-speaking informants who initially had claimed to be Catalan on the basis of birthplace excluded themselves from and contrasted themselves to the Catalan group in further discussion. When questioned about these actual uses of "Catalan" here, they often responded that they were now talking about "Catalan Catalans," making it clear that when discussing the traits, behavior, and attitudes of Catalans, they meant Catalan speakers. Catalan speakers themselves used the "Catalan" label almost exclusively to refer to Catalan speakers.

At the public level, one of the Catalan government's language planners wrote the following critical commentary on a survey conducted by the Socialist Party:

They tell us that 55% of the Andalusians feel Catalan, but only 20% of the Andalusians know how to speak Catalan! With the rest of the immigrants, it is the same: 63% feel themselves to be Catalan, but only 39% know how to speak Catalan. This doesn't help to make it understood that a Catalan knows how to speak Catalan. If he doesn't, many people would not even consider him as such. Again, we see how some politicians foment . . . "a crisis in the concept of Catalan identity"! (Strubell i Trueta 1980)

The overt debate over who is Catalan was as rare in daily life (when unprobed by the questioning ethnographer) as it was common in the media during this period. People usually did not argue about their identities, they performed them. Attempts to regularize ethnicity, to use Moore's (1975) term, and therefore regularize social relations, are made principally by political and public figures, but people used these regularities every day to accomplish interactional goals. Occasionally, ethnic debate did arise in interaction, usually as a recourse in another conflict. And when it did, in face-to-face interaction as in public commentary, the linguistic criterion overrode all other claims to Catalan identity.

An unusually bald example is an argument that erupted between a Catalan-speaking teacher and her roomer's dinner guest, a young Castilian-speaking worker born in Barcelona of Andalusian parents. Hot debate over the explanation of economic problems led to argument over Catalan ethnocentrism, which the worker invoked in a clichéd form. To claim his right to this opinion, the young man said in Castilian, "I'm Catalan." The teacher flatly returned that he was not. He insisted that he was Catalan, although "perhaps not by the accent," and she again denied it, "not because of the accent, but the words." This declaration effectively ended all debate, the young man's right to criticize Catalans publicly rejected along with his claim to Catalan identity.

Other Identities

If not everyone is Catalan, who else can one be in Barcelona? One answer that I received to this question from a working-class Catalan teenager was, "There are only three kinds of people in Barcelona: Catalans, foreigners from Spain, and foreigners from outside of Spain." Although this reveals the potential strength of Catalanist feeling, it is an extreme rhetorical position. Many other possible identities are recognized by various segments of the population.

First, group affiliation can be derived from other regions of Spain—for example Murcian, Extremaduran, Galician, Aragonese, or Andalusian. These identities are usually claimed or attributed because one was born in the region named, but occasionally because one's parents were born there. Immigrants may be very literal in their application of this definition. A young domestic worker insisted that both her Castilian-speaking husband and her children were Catalan, since they had been born in Barcelona, but she herself was Andalusian because she had been born in Seville and brought to Barcelona at the age of four months. Several adult education students who had immigrated to Catalonia as children reported that they always say they are Andalusian or Murcian, never Catalan. They feel no tie to their native lands and claim a strong emotional commitment to Catalonia; some have never revisited their home regions and have no desire to do so. Nonetheless, they scrupulously claimed their birth identity, perhaps partly to show they are unashamed of their origins and partly to avoid being considered presumptuous for claiming to be Catalan.

Two of these regional terms have a second, more general use. Even those who have no tie to Andalusia or Murcia may be called Andalusians or Murcians, and more infrequently may even refer to themselves as such. Since the early waves of immigration came mainly from Murcia, all working-class Castilian-speaking immigrants came to be referred to as Murcians by extension, and this habit lingers in some sectors. Older immigrants (including one from Murcia) remember this as an extremely disdainful insult, and recall instances when they suffered it. Since Murcia was largely replaced by Andalusia as the source of immigration in the 1960's, so was the term Murcian replaced by Andalusian as a general means of referring to all working-class Castilian speakers in Catalonia, often derogatorily.

"Immigrant" itself is a cover term commonly used to refer to non-Catalans in Catalonia. In addition to geographical origin, the term encodes a class distinction and is only used in reference to working-class non-Catalans. An important epithet for the same group is the highly charged term **xarnego**. Of uncertain but apparently innocent etymology, it reputedly originally referred to a Catalan whose parents came from different valleys. The meaning was extended and came to focus on people who have one Catalan and one non-Catalan parent; some say more specifically a Catalan and a French parent. More generally, it was used to refer to people of non-Catalan origin residing in Catalonia, and especially native-born Castilian speakers. The term has class as well as ethnic connotations; like "Andalusian" and "Murcian," it refers only to working-class Castilian speakers, not to the governmental or business-management personnel who came to Barcelona after the war years. Highly derogatory and insulting, **xarnego** was a word known to all but rarely spoken publicly in 1979–80. Except for occasional muttered remarks by Catalan speakers, the term was used almost exclusively by immigrants themselves, either jokingly or in aggressive assertion of their status. An author and political figure described himself as a "**xarnego** author" (Candel 1977); an anti-Catalanist writer belittled him as an example of the "grateful **xarnego**" syndrome (Jiménez Losantos 1979).

The most commonly used term for non-Catalan identity is "Castilian" (**castellà**, *castellano*), used by Catalans and non-Catalans alike. Differentiation between Catalans and Castilians is the dominant mode of ethnic classification in Barcelona. Like "Catalan," "Castilian" is basically a language-determined identity. As a Catalan is one whose native and habitual language is Catalan, so a Castilian is a person whose native and habitual language is Castilian.

In origin, "Castilian" is another region-based term, referring to

Castile, the location of Madrid and the heartland of Spain. But the Spanish language is known in Iberia as Castilian and, by extension, "Castilian" has come to refer to all Castilian speakers, regardless of region of origin.

The contrast between Catalans and Castilians *within* Catalan society is the tension-provoking pervasive dichotomy that politicians seek to eradicate. Many leaders object vigorously to any reference to "two communities" or "two cultures" in Catalonia. Some claim to see Catalonia as one community that expresses itself in two languages. Others point out that Catalonia now comprises many communities, as the variety of region-based identity terms demonstrates; they deny the cultural unity of the Castilian speakers (Moll 1981). Nonetheless, the two terms Catalan and Castilian are used as an exhaustive contrast set by the overwhelming majority of individuals in Barcelona. Castilian identity in Catalonia is built upon and subsumes, rather than contrasts to, immigrant regional identities such as Andalusian or Murcian. Unlike other extended uses of regional terms, it also encompasses elites and professionals as well as workers, making it from the dominant Catalanist political viewpoint a particularly dangerous comprehensive category.

Evans-Pritchard (1940) demonstrated how in the segmentary structure of a society, groups that contrast to one another in one context may be united in another; this observation has since proved useful in understanding modern ethnicity (Despres 1975b, Cohen 1974a). In Catalonia, a unitary Castilian identity emerges from more restricted local identities in the social process of immigrant interaction with a self-conscious Catalan community that defines itself through its language. This process demonstrates an important aspect of modern ethnicity, that it is not simply the result of cultural conservatism and isolation, but rather the outcome of intensive interaction (Cohen 1974a: 96–97). Castilian as a language-based identity is meaningful in contrast to Catalan identity; each takes its significance from the overall pattern of opposition, rather than simply in relation to a particular homeland or its customs.

Even those who are in sympathy with Catalan nationalist political goals find it difficult to employ the all-inclusive definition of Catalans and to avoid a basic dichotomy, not so much of Catalans and Castilians as of native-born and (working-class) immigrant, which the political definition attempts to abolish. The differences in class, access to institutional resources, and quality of life that coincide with this division are too significant to be easily ignored. In any extended or serious discussion of the social and economic situation of Catalonia, the dichotomy inevitably must surface, and various means are used to index it.

At public events such as campaign rallies or scholarly conferences, the vocabulary of differentiation is circumspect, and the contrast between "Catalans" and "immigrants," or "Catalans" and "Castilians" is often avoided. In its place, people may speak of Catalans and "other Catalans," drawing on the title of a best-selling book on immigration from the 1960's (Candel 1964). As happens to most euphemisms over time, this one has become transparent and has taken on some of the pejorative connotations of the term it replaces. Thus in 1979–80 one came to hear of "Catalans of origin," "old Catalans," or "Those who have always been Catalan" (**catalans de sempre**) in contrast to "Catalans of immigration," "new Catalans," "Catalans of adoption," "recent Catalans," and "newcomer Catalans." Users of these euphemisms attempted to remain within the unitary framework of the slogan "all those who live and work here are Catalan," yet still address a significant division in the population. However, such euphemisms have not taken root in the vocabulary of private and everyday discourse. Informants from both groups readily discussed the life of their city in terms of Catalans and Castilians.

Another term at issue is *español* (**espanyol**; Spanish or Spaniard). Most "old Catalans" do not identify at all with the term, many would never use it for themselves, and some reject it vehemently. In a public meeting, an impassioned young man accused a Catalan presidential candidate of moral compromise and political bankruptcy, because he endorsed a Statute of Autonomy that "says we are Spaniards." When "new Catalans" are asked if they are Spanish, on the other hand, the answer will most often be "yes," even for those who have become bilingual or identify themselves as Catalan as well. Shabad and Gunther (1982) found that only 19 percent of native Catalan speakers consider themselves primarily Spanish, whereas 66 percent of non-native Catalan speakers give this identity and 84 percent of monolingual Castilian speakers in Catalonia accept this designation.

The most nationalist Catalans as well as the most nationalist Spaniards carry the process of segmentary opposition to its logical conclusion, explicitly identifying the Castilian immigrant within Catalonia and the external Spanish opponent in a single category of Spaniards contrasting to Catalans. It is precisely this association between Castilian ethnolinguistic identity and Spanish political identity that moderate leaders fear most, and it seemed unthinkable to them that Catalans would publicly suggest such a connection. To call immigrants "**espanyols**" is tantamount to accusing them of being representatives and advocates of centralist Spanish domination and enemies of Catalonia. In a highly provocative article entitled, "A Nation Without a State, a People Without a Language?" a group of Catalan intellectuals challenged the politicians' position and endorsed this Catalan-Spanish contrast: "The last step in (the) process of the taboo-ization of the term Catalan—to the disadvantage of Catalans and in favor of the Spaniards—is that used, significantly, by the one who in theory holds the greatest responsibility in Catalan politics, when he used the term 'Citizens of Catalonia.' Presumably he did this in order not to offend the sensibilities of the Spaniards" (Argente et al. 1979; my translation).

In some lights, the flurry (and fury) of public definitional activity seems a formalistic and sterile exercise. Why the many public commentaries on "who is Catalan" when no civil rights or obligations are distributed according to ethnic identity in this society? Moore has referred to this kind of activity as "regularization" (1975: 219). By invoking normative categories for talking about social relations and attempting to regularize these, or to place a particular interpretation on their inherent ambiguities, participants attempt to order those social relations themselves. Debating over who can and should claim Catalan identity is a symbolic act that indirectly articulates and summarizes positions on more concrete issues: the right to make critical commentary with impunity, the socioeconomic shape of any "new Catalonia," the power of particular elites, the political status of Catalonia, the fate of the Catalan language.

Ethnic Boundaries and Group Stereotypes

The ethnic differences indexed by language are significant in interpersonal politics as well as national politics, because people believe they accompany culturally determined group differences in outlook, personality, and behavior. The primary social boundary marked by language is reinforced by stereotyped images of each group.

Although not everyone in Barcelona prefers to talk in terms of ethnic stereotypes, these clichés are such a central part of folk wisdom that they were volunteered to me repeatedly by strangers on trains or park benches as well as by informants in interviews. Catalans are often characterized as ambitious, intelligent, sensible, industrious people, by both insiders and outsiders. Catalans themselves are very proud of what they see as one of their most traditional traits, **seny**. Literally "sense," it refers to levelheaded, feet-on-the-ground common sense. There is an extensive native literature exploring and extolling this aspect of the national character, as well as other facets such as the unity of the family, religious devotion, the work ethic, and **pactisme**, the time-honored Catalan tradition of negotiation and compromise (Solé-Tura 1974).

More negatively, Catalans are often stereotyped as cold, closed, unfriendly, ungenerous, and miserly. Jokes about this last trait abound and are often told by Catalans themselves. Immigrants who are bitter about their experiences in Catalonia often focus on what they see as mean-spiritedness and haughtiness in Catalans, but even those who feel more positively toward Catalans also mention the coldness and closed nature of the Catalan personality. They hasten to add, however, that once Catalans have accepted a friend, they will be unstintingly loyal and generous, more reliable and trustworthy than the Castilian, who makes friends more easily.

There are variations in the stereotype of Castilians, depending on whether the prototypical member is taken to be the urban Madrileño from Castile or the Andalusian immigrant. But shared characteristics of these images include an expansive nature, immediate openness and friendliness, good humor, demonstrativeness, and generosity, both financial and moral. The negative counterparts of this image include gladhanding, boastfulness, loudness, and laziness.

These stereotypes are no doubt familiar, even banal, to many who have worked in a stratified society; their counterparts can be found easily in the United States, for example. Indeed, class and rural-urban differences provide important bases for these ethnic images in Catalonia. Conceptions of the Catalan character were most fully formulated in reference to the nineteenth-century bourgeoisie and what Giner calls "that most Catalan of social classes," the **menestralia**, made up of artisans and shopkeepers (1984: 17), and it has been difficult to extricate Catalan identity from this bourgeois background. This is the task faced by leftist Catalan leaders in contemporary politics; Hansen (1977) has called it a fatal paradox of nationalist political mobilization.

Ethnic stereotypes function and are maintained in spite of, or perhaps even because of, the permeability of group boundaries (Barth 1969). The process of permeation actually serves to confirm them, much as class-based stereotypes are confirmed in the United States by Horatio Alger instances of upward social mobility. Thus a Castilian-speaking immigrant who invests the effort in learning to speak Catalan in a native-like fashion despite the adverse conditions of the post–Civil War period is thought to demonstrate the hardworking ambition, good sense, and long-range goal orientation that qualify one as a genuine Catalan.

For example, Maria, a middle-aged immigrant worker, is considered by her peers to be more Catalan than Castilian. She reported that upon arriving in Barcelona as children, she and her brother consciously decided to become Catalans. They spoke only Catalan outside of the home, and she was so adamant about her affiliation that she would dance only with Catalan boys; she once left a fellow on the dance floor upon discovering that he spoke Castilian.

As a young woman, Maria was able to get a supervisory position in a textile factory. Upon hearing that two more such positions were open, she sent two Castilian-speaking neighbors to interview with her boss. When they did not get the positions, she asked him why and was told it was because they were Castilians. When she pointed out that she too was Castilian, her boss replied, "You're different."

This informant's account of an earlier time demonstrates the social reality of the group boundary as much as its permeability. The essence of the manipulation of identity symbols like language is that such symbols constitute claims to be judged by the standards relevant to that identity (Barth 1969: 15–16). There is little doubt that this woman was accepted as virtually Catalan by her boss, but there is also little doubt that through her language shift she had demonstrated personal traits that in his view both set her off from the Castilian-speaking peers and qualified her for a position of responsibility. Categorical ethnic distinctions, especially as they coincide with class distinctions, do not depend on an absence of mobility, but are maintained despite changing participation and membership in the course of individual life histories (ibid.: 19).

What Difference Does It Make?

As Maria's story indicates, ethnic identity can carry important consequences for the life chances of individuals in the Barcelona area. Informants agreed that incidents of anti-immigrant discrimination in the workplace occurred in the earlier postwar years, though they felt that these had diminished in the 1970's. Solé and Vicens (1979) found that only nine of 520 interviewees felt language to be a discriminatory factor in the workplace. (In the view of some Castilian speakers, however, in 1980, a new kind of discrimination was on the rise under the auspices of the new Catalan government and a pro-Catalan linguistic policy.)

There is a strong association between origin, and therefore language group, and occupation, residence, and educational opportunities (see Figs. 2.1 and 2.2). Straightforward discrimination, however, has been perhaps the least critical foundation of these differences, given the educational disparities between the native and immigrant sectors. Solé (1982: 28–29) found that approximately 30 percent of immigrant workers had no education at all, whereas this was true of only 9 percent of Catalan-born workers. All of the immigrants she interviewed recognized that educational and professional qualifications were the greatest determinants of job possibilities, and immigrants experience considerable occupational mobility relative to native-borns (albeit within lower occupational ranks). It has been shown, however, that the qualified immigrant has a lower chance of employment in mid- and upper-level positions in smaller businesses than in large ones (Pinilla de las Heras 1979). This bias is significant, since small family businesses are characteristic of Catalonia; of 140,000 firms, only 1.1 percent have more than 200 employees (Caraben Ribó 1982).

Occupational and residential segregation has had important consequences for the solidification of the ethnic distinction between the two groups. Demographic studies have shown that the concentration of immigrants in suburban dormitory cities is associated with a significant tendency toward endogamous Castilian and endogamous Catalan marriages (Pinilla de las Heras 1979). And even where the

low occupational status of immigrants is warranted by lack of training and skills, its effects on the life opportunities of succeeding generations create considerable danger that the coincidence of class and
ethnic divisions will be exacerbated, not alleviated, over time (cf.
Solé and Vicens 1979).

Not everyone in Barcelona believes that there are cultural differences between the groups; some informants claimed that, apart from
the first immigrant generation, there are no real differences in "way
of life" between Catalans and Castilians in Barcelona. Others tabu-
lated long lists of differences that went well beyond the basic stereotypes, from facial expressions to styles of dress and manner of walking. But even those who rejected the idea of cultural differences recognized important social differences. "Here's where the difference
begins," said one Castilian student as we stood at the gate of his
school. He was pointing to a lone Catalan classmate, heading home
in one direction while his Castilian classmates were taking the other.

Among the consequences of this coincidence of class and ethnic
boundaries are the personal dilemmas that possibilities or aspirations for mobility can provoke. Catalans themselves do not often experience what might be thought of as identity conflict. On the contrary, most seem quite secure in their knowledge of themselves as
Catalans and proud of this identity, even though they may bitterly
resent the treatment Catalonia has received from Madrid.

However, the immigrant and the immigrant's child face conflicting demands on their loyalty and conflicting pressures on their self-
definition. The ambitions for social advance that led them to emi-
grate in the first place encourage the immigrants, when confronted
with the class differential between Castilians and Catalans, to try to
"catalanize" themselves. But their social separation from Catalans
and their resulting dependency on the support of Castilian networks,
their perceptions of discrimination, and a defensive reaction to the
Catalan habit of viewing Castilians as the political adversary, all create counterpressures that favor maintenance and even emphasis of a
Castilian identity (cf. Solé 1987).

The responses of immigrants to these conflicting pressures on
identity are diverse, and by no means do all those of immigrant origin
experience irresolvable difficulties. Many, however, are troubled by
the ethnic dichotomy and unable to find a comfortable solution to
conflicting claims on their allegiance. There is no one immigrant or

Castilian experience in Catalonia, nor is there a single response to that experience, but there are regular, recurring dimensions to the problem of identity. Thumbnail sketches of several immigrant-origin informants, representing a spectrum of understandings of and responses to the challenges of identity, will illustrate both the variety and the regularities.

Handling Identity Dilemmas: Some Examples

Puri. Some informants appear to be untouched by ethnic identity problems. Puri is a young immigrant from Galicia who is a domestic worker in Catalan houses, as are her mother and sister. She is engaged to be married to a Catalan whose parents, themselves of working-class origin, own a very small commercial business in a peripheral neighborhood. Puri recalls no particular ethnic difficulties in Barcelona since her arrival at age eight, and she is nonchalant about the polemics raging over identity issues. The only time she reported ever having to confront group stereotypes was with her brother, who emigrated to Switzerland shortly after Puri came to Barcelona. He and his friends accuse Catalan men of loose morals and unfaithfulness to their spouses. Confronted with such prejudiced taunts, she moved quickly to defend Catalans and her future husband. But she herself has no strong feeling of being either Catalan or Castilian, and no conviction of important differences between the groups. Puri speaks no Catalan, and is consistently addressed in Castilian by her future husband and in-laws, although she understands Catalan well. She plans to speak Castilian to her children and assumes that they will learn Catalan from their father.

Consuelo, Rosa, Maria Teresa, and Soledad. These women all immigrated as children from the south of Spain, two with their families, and two on their own as domestic laborers. All began working as servants or in factories by the age of thirteen, and all have experienced poverty and the hardships of immigration. Only now, as married women in their twenties and thirties, are they completing their elementary educations. Only one of the four speaks Catalan with any regularity, and all are very clear and frank about their non-Catalan origins and identity. None claims to *be* Catalan, but all claim to *feel* much more Catalan than Andalusian or Murcian. They either do not know their homelands or remember them with distaste. Each feels well integrated into Catalonia, and each reports a warm remembrance of the kindness of Catalans during her childhood.

One recalls puddings and cookies at the home of a Catalan sewing instructor when her own family was too poor to feed all the children well; another remembers a young Catalan woman who would get up in the middle of the night to escort her immigrant neighbor to a factory job; the third tells of the Catalan family next door who found employment for both her father and her brother at a time when each new worker had to be spoken for. Soledad recalls being so small and underweight at thirteen, when she was hired to care for a Catalan child, that the mother ended up caring for both of them, treating her as a daughter. Perhaps the most pathetic story of all is that of the young woman who still remembers with deep gratitude the sandwich she was given by her new Catalan employers when she arrived hungry and tired from the south to work as a servant in their home.

These reminiscences range from the humorous to the pathetic, and certainly might be said to exemplify the "grateful **xarnego**" syndrome rejected by Jiménez Losantos. But they all are etched in the memories of these women, having affected them deeply, and they are a significant factor in both their interpersonal relations and their political responses to Catalan nationalism. Two of the women are active members of the Catalan Communist Party (PSUC), endorsing both its class and its Catalanist programs. At the same time that these women are unashamed of their Castilian identities, they are highly loyal to Catalans and Catalonia. Nonetheless, they believe catalanization, for example in job requirements, must proceed slowly to avoid discrimination and injustice to working-class Castilians.

Reyes. For other informants, the issue of identity is more conflictive and demands a choice in favor of one group, a rejection of the other. Reyes, a classmate of the four women discussed above, is deeply embittered by her experiences in Catalonia. She arrived in Barcelona at thirteen to work as a servant. Reyes is resentful of Catalans, and all her reminiscences served to illustrate Catalans' attitude of superiority, their class and ethnic snobbery, and their lack of generosity toward the immigrants who she believes are equally, if not more, responsible for building the Catalonia in which they all live. (This last sentiment is a common refrain among many immigrants.) Reyes believes that all Catalans resent the intrusion of Castilians, and that they are now vengefully trying to force immigrants to give up their identity and culture; however, she is markedly apolitical and does not translate this analysis into political action. Unlike her co-workers, she professes great nostalgia for her *tierra* (land) and her *pueblo* (town, people). After twenty-three years of residence in Catalonia, she still wishes she could return to Andalusia, although she recognizes that she would now be unhappy with the standard of living there. Unlike her companions, Reyes speaks no Catalan at all and speaks Castilian with a strong Andalusian accent.

Pep. The son of immigrants from a northern agricultural region of Spain, twenty-three-year-old Pep has had different opportunities and has chosen the ethnic path opposite that taken by Reyes. Brought to a provincial city of the Barcelona area as a child by his working-class parents, he was raised in a Castilian-speaking household and had mostly Castilian friends throughout school. He did not begin to speak Catalan until he left home to attend university in Barcelona, but now it is his preferred, habitual language, and he uses the Catalan form of his name. Pep is a member of a nationalist, leftist, nonparliamentary Catalan party. He was reluctant to discuss his ethnic transformation with me, claiming that to become catalanized was the most natural and logical course, in need of no explanation or exploration. Like many Catalans, he cringes at the mention of bullfights and despises flamenco, which he rejects as importations of Spanish culture having no place in Catalonia except to remind Catalans of their oppression.

Like Reyes, Pep holds no stock in the integration of two cultures in Catalonia. His view of the problem, however, is very different. Pep believes firmly that Catalonia must not become a melting pot with a melded culture; the new Catalonia must be faithful to the true Catalan language and culture or not be at all. In his insistence he was more vehement than many native Catalans. Pep has chosen to embrace fully a Catalan identity and to reject his Castilian identity of origin, and he believes assimilation is the choice that all immigrants must make.

Ignacio. Other informants experienced, or at least were more willing to admit to, confusion and ambivalent allegiance. Ignacio is a sixteen-year-old public school student in an immigrant ghetto, the son of Murcian workers. He is representative of many second-generation immigrants in using the birthplace criterion to define himself as Catalan. Since he was born in Catalonia, Ignacio claims to have no doubt that he is Catalan. But in a two-hour discussion about his life and conditions in Barcelona, he referred to himself as Castilian, Murcian, and even Andalusian, and not once did he group himself with Catalans.

Ignacio's changing self-categorization indicates that some identities are more appropriate to certain kinds of talk; though the setting and participants did not change, the focus of Ignacio's remarks did change in the discussion, from politics (in which he was "Andalusian") to linguistic discrimination ("Castilian") to life in the neighborhood ("Murcian"), etc. But in spite of the appropriateness of some of this variation, Ignacio also expressed insecurity about his identity. He reported feeling awkward when talking to people from outside of Catalonia and defining himself as Catalan, since he does not speak the language or identify with Catalan folkloric customs or history. He summed it up by saying that he knows he is Catalan, but that he does not feel it, and he wonders if he is somehow at fault for this.

Josefina. A classmate of Ignacio's, Josefina has a very different response to the situation. When she was eight, she came to Barcelona from Albacete, a province near Murcia (where Ignacio's parents are from). Josefina offers the same definition of Catalan identity as Ignacio. That is, she knows she is not Catalan, because she was not born in Catalonia, but she considers people like Ignacio Catalan because they were born there. The difference is that not only does she give this definition, she also uses it. The contrast between those born in Catalonia and those born outside is meaningful to her. References to Catalans in her conversation frequently contrasted all natives of Catalonia, regardless of language, to those from outside; most of the contrasts she drew were favorable to Catalans.

Whereas Ignacio knows he is Catalan but does not feel it, Josefina says she knows she is not Catalan but feels as if she were. Immigrants' ties to the homeland do not necessarily function to help them maintain identification with the region of origin. For Josefina, the experience of returning to her birthplace was one of shock that led to a solidification of her feelings of Catalan identity. In her Albacete village she was teased by former friends as "La Catalana," and she was not accepted back into her old circle on an equal footing. This teasing combines rejection and respect; Josefina was at least partly proud of the label. And it was after being teased as a Catalan in her native village that Josefina decided that her identity in Barcelona as "La Albacetina" was untenable. Upon her return to Barcelona she began efforts to learn the Catalan language, to get to know Catalan-speaking people, and to transform herself into a Catalan. She was still in the process at the time we met.

Helena. A young university-educated woman in her mid-twenties, Helena is the daughter of a Murcian mother and a Castilian-speaking father born in Catalonia. Raised in Barcelona in a middle-class home, she learned Catalan as a teenager and later married a Catalan with whom she worked. Their relationship has always been conducted in Catalan, and Helena speaks Catalan to their two children. She is comfortable in the language and uses it without problems with her husband's family and friends. Nonetheless, Helena passes through periods of disenchantment and even rejection of the Catalan language and culture, and at the time of our extended interview she found herself in one of these. She felt that between her husband Joan and herself there was "not an integration, but a confrontation of two cultures." In domestic arguments, each takes the part of his and her own ethnic group, belittling the other. Helena may criticize Catalan literature or speak of historical events, but these, she believes, are a means of hiding her "nonintegration into the Catalan world." She has, in her own words, "a will, I believe conscious, not to let myself be eaten by the Catalans."

Helena is disturbed that her children are not learning Castilian: "I don't want them to take that away from me." But she nonetheless feels "ridiculous" and "unnatural" speaking Castilian to her baby. Helena thinks that at times she deliberately speaks Catalan poorly, as a last resort. "Sometimes I'm afraid that they've already beaten me, that one day I'll find myself thinking in Catalan. Maybe this resistance to the language is a fear of losing my own Castilian identity." When she begins to feel she has lost her own world, she imposes her Castilian language more on her husband and his friends: "It's always a little bit like a war. And I don't know up to what point it's a game, or actually hides the reality of a person who has not integrated herself into a culture."

When I asked Helena what "Catalan culture" meant to her, she laughingly responded "the enemy," and in her skirmishes with her husband, she sees herself as the defender of Castilian culture, which is being "systematically massacred by the Catalans." By her own admission, her defensive stance is objectively unwarranted and "completely out of place," since she recognizes and sympathizes with Catalan political goals generally. Nonetheless she defends Castilian high culture; "I won't let them eat it away." She is acutely conscious of the use of the Catalan language as a political weapon and resents the implication that as a Castilian speaker she is an enemy. When she perceives the Catalan language to be used for political purposes, a symbol of nationalist demands for justice, Helena as a Castilian speaker feels it as a weapon of oppression.

It is unlikely that Helena would always express such strong anti-Catalan feelings, even to an outsider; it is more probable that her ambivalence about language and identity was accentuated by domestic problems between herself and her husband in a period of adjustment to new living circumstances. Nonetheless, it is evident that ethnicity is a latent, though not always active, issue in their interpersonal struggles. It underlies their relationship as both an impediment and a resource in strategic maneuvers, always ready to surface to turn an interpersonal problem into an interethnic one.

Ana. Similar personal conflicts and their interaction with larger political processes are illustrated in the story of Ana, an unemployed clerical worker. Thirty years old, she had come at age ten from a poor farm family in a rural region of Castile to a convent school in the center of Barcelona, where she learned to speak Catalan with native-like ability.

During the year that I knew her, Ana passed through several stages in the definition of her own identity. Before the political campaigning for the referendum began in the city, she was very proud of both her Castilian origins and the extent to which she had catalanized herself. Yet as the campaign for Catalan autonomy heated up, she encountered serious problems, and the referendum put into question her capacity to be loyal to both groups. Ana and her Castilian guests began to have arguments with her Catalan roommates over political, linguistic, and economic rights in the new Catalonia. About the same time Ana shifted from characterizing these roommates as polite and reserved ("very Catalan, very nice") to selfish, ungenerous, haughty, and close-minded ("typically Catalan").

When Ana changed apartments, however, and acquired Castilian-speaking roommates from various parts of Spain, she told me she now realized that she was really more Catalan than Castilian. She no longer felt "at home" in a Castilian-speaking household. Ana was uncomfortable with her new roommates, and characterized them as

lazy, dirty, intellectually uncurious dropouts—in short, "Castilians."
I questioned these generalizations about Castilian speakers, and suggested that the differences between Ana and her roommates could be due more to their age and social situation than their origins or language group. Ana stood by her claim that a very basic difference in the outlook of Catalans and Castilians was at issue. Again, I suggested that it was a difference that was due more to urban and industrial life than to ethnicity. Ana rejected this, too, claiming that even a Catalan peasant is more intellectually alert than most Castilians, and illustrating her claim with a story of a rural gentleman she once met. It was during this period that Ana first began to use the words "we" and "ours" when referring to Catalans and things Catalan; before, she had always been sympathetic to the Catalan cause but was careful never to characterize herself as a member of the group.

Ana is obviously a person who thinks in terms of unusually strong stereotypes. When I left Barcelona, she had still not settled the question of which group she belonged to, and her solution was to plan to move away from Catalonia. For reasons of personal history, she was probably destined to be a marginal woman in many ways—she aspired to a level of success that her educational preparation would not easily allow her. What is important is that she so frequently phrased her personal problems in terms of a cultural confrontation between what she saw as two very distinct and mutually exclusive groups in Barcelona, each with some traits that she valued and others that she despised.

It should not be concluded from these last examples that social networks cannot cross ethnic boundaries in Barcelona, but rather that there is a boundary that constrains relations, a boundary that must be implicitly or explicitly recognized when it is crossed. Stable, persisting, and important social relations are often maintained across such boundaries (Barth 1969: 19), and many people have formed successful intimate relations across these group lines in Barcelona. But even those who have done so must at times contend with difficulties in which culture and politics are intertwined.

Ethnic Identity and the Nation-State

Since the death of Franco and the opening of possibilities for political change, the primary political interest in Catalonia has been in minimizing the internal ethnic and class boundary that Ana has elevated to a guiding principle of her life. The political dilemma of ethnicity in Catalonia is no less difficult than the personal dilemma, in the sense that leaders are simultaneously attempting two contrary processes associated with nation-state building. Vis-à-vis Madrid, Catalonia's leaders are engaged in a limited form of state building through the politicization of ethnicity, claiming that because it is a distinct nation, Catalonia merits the right to administer its own affairs. But within Catalonia, they find themselves simultaneously involved in nation building, or the ethnicization of polity, attempting to convince the immigrant-origin working class that it too is Catalan in contrast to other Spaniards.

The ambiguity of the often-heard phrase "national reconstruction of Catalonia" is evidence of this dual process. To some, the phrase calls for the establishment of democratic political institutions that respond to the social and economic needs of the population of Catalonia, as was not done under the Franco government. Political and economic rather than cultural reconstruction is implied. To others, however, the phrase is primarily a call for the restoration of a specifically Catalan character and culture for the territory. The differences between the two camps are usually revealed when the fate desired for the immigrant population is discussed, as for example in a public conference on "Immigration and National Reconstruction" in the fall of 1979. Proponents of the first interpretation spoke of the "integration" of immigrants into Catalan life, and particularly economic life, while the second view held that cultural "assimilation" of the immigrants was the major task in national reconstruction.

When the boundary between Spain as a whole and Catalonia as an autonomous nation within it is to be emphasized and legitimized, the population of Catalonia must understand itself as internally homogeneous, in some essential way "the same" in contrast to the rest of the peoples of Spain. But because of the identification of Spain with Castile, and the reliance on language as a key political symbol, moves to reinforce the boundary between Catalans and Spaniards at the state level paradoxically exacerbate the polarization of groups within Catalonia (cf. Linz 1975: 374–75). The Castilian or Spanish political adversary of Catalonia is often acknowledged to be different from the Castilian immigrant in Catalonia, but both are symbolized by the same language and referred to by the same term. It is therefore not entirely surprising that efforts to champion the cause of Catalans and

Catalan, ostensibly vis-à-vis Madrid, are met with the solidification of self-conscious and defensive Castilian identity *within* Catalonia.

In 1979, the leading political parties compromised the nation- and state-building processes through a provisional de-ethnicization of identity. Campaign slogans emptied Catalan identity of its contrastive linguistic and cultural content within Catalonia, making it more a civic than an ethnic identity. Yet de-ethnicizing Catalan identity was anathema to many native Catalans and undermined the moral basis of the state imperative. The possibility of restoring the cultural and linguistic content of Catalan identity after political boundaries were secured was viewed as an empty promise by many Catalans and as a real threat by many Castilians. Neither group seemed particularly secure or happy with this resolution of the two opposing processes.

The fact that the contemporary political goal has been autonomy within the Spanish state rather than total independence has meant that in Geertz's (1973) schema, the first, or "independence movement," phase of Catalan nationalism can never be said to have terminated. Although former colonies such as India confront many problems, the fear that England will move back in and once again take administrative control is not one of these. But for Catalonia, autonomous status is granted by the Spanish government, and can be amended or withdrawn if the Spanish government determines that such a step is in the general interest of the state (Clark 1980: 98). The passing of a Statute of Autonomy is therefore not an assurance that the "independence" phase is completed. Within memory, Catalonia has seen itself stripped of hard-won autonomous powers. In the existing framework of the Constitution and the Statute of Autonomy, Catalan leaders must negotiate continually with the power of Madrid to define, extend, and defend the domain of their administrative authority.*

Thus as Catalonia moved into the difficult second phase faced by "new nations," the definition of its internal social and cultural character, it had to continue to guard its border with Madrid. In effect, the people of Catalonia are required to operate simultaneously

---

*That this continues to be the case was demonstrated by debates held in the Catalan Parlament in February 1987 over the inadequacy of the Statute and of the Spanish Socialist government's application of it. Taylor's discussion of the repercussions of the Ley Orgánica de Armonización del Proceso Autonómico (LOAPA) of 1982 gives another important example of this persisting tension (1983: 3–4).

within two frames for knowing who they are. Such a necessity places constraints on the negotiation of a definition of Catalan society, some to the advantage of current leaders and some to their disadvantage.

Not only must Catalonia simultaneously play out two phases of nationalism that are usually played sequentially, but in both struggles, only the same limited set of cultural symbols and ethnic alternatives are available. It is as if two games were being played with the same ball. Again in comparison to the example of India, one of the most ethnically complicated of postcolonial states, the ethnic situation in Catalonia can be seen to be unusually involuted.

In India, the two phases of nationalist activity—difficult and virulent as each may be—have been articulated in separate frameworks of dichotomization and differentiation, each drawn from a different grid of possibilities. In the early stages, it was possible to define the struggle as one of India against the English, and to ignore to a large extent the problem of what being Indian might actually mean. In the second phase, when it became necessary to define the character of the Indian state, the groups that mobilized for action were drawn from a different grid. With the English retired from action, it has become a question of Telegu against Tamil, Tamil in competition with Hindi, etc., in so different a frame of contrast that in compromise, English can be accepted as a language of wider communication (Geertz 1973, Inglehart and Woodward 1972).

In Catalonia, however, the definition of external boundaries and the definition of internal character involve the same basic identities and symbols; it becomes very difficult to keep their meanings in the two different struggles separate. The struggle with the central government is one of Catalans against Castilians; the competition within Catalonia to define the nature of Catalan society is also one of Catalans and Castilians. Though the two processes are distinct, motivated by different forces, they take place simultaneously, crosscutting each other, and with recourse to the same restricted set of symbols, undercutting each other.

It is at least in part because of this dual frame for interpreting personal experience that people can "feel Catalan" but not "be Catalan" at one and the same time, or find that they are Catalan but not "Catalan Catalan," as many express it. Of course, although there may be two analytically distinct processes of ethnic differentiation operating in Barcelona, in each case there is only one individual who must make decisions about and on the basis of his or her identity.

Where the contexts can be held in focus separately, different criteria and symbols of identity can be foregrounded at different times. But since the processes of differentiation (of Catalonia within Castilian Spain, of Catalans and Castilians within Catalonia) are evolving simultaneously, they are often experienced as conflicting by the individual and resolved in the varying and ad hoc manners described in this chapter. Although individuals may in fact be responding to two different sets of pressures in their various moves, they can never be assured that all parties are invoking the same frame for interpreting their signals. Conflict and ambivalence such as that felt by Ana result not simply from psychological constraints that make it difficult to uproot one's inculcated identity, but from contradictions between two different epistemological frames for knowing who one is provided by the social and political structure of Catalonia and the Spanish state.

CHAPTER FOUR RIGHTS AND DUTIES
OF LANGUAGE
CHOICE

In the preceding chapter we saw that ethnic identity in Barcelona depends on language use as a key determinant of group membership. People are identified as Catalan or Castilian, most often on the basis of whether they are "Catalan speakers" (**catalanoparlants,** *catalanohablantes*) or "Castilian speakers" (**castellanoparlants,** *castellanohablantes*). Although these linguistic diagnostics are those used in Barcelona, they may mislead the outsider inasmuch as they evoke an image of two contrasting monolingual groups. Owing to historical circumstances, nearly all Catalan speakers in Barcelona are bilingual, fully proficient in Castilian, and many use Castilian in their daily routines. Moreover, it is estimated that 25 percent to 30 percent of Castilian speakers actively employ Catalan on some occasions (Strubell i Trueta 1981a).* Thus the labels "Catalan"/"Catalan speaker" and "Castilian"/"Castilian speaker" do not reflect the entire linguistic repertoire of the individual, but simply indicate the active use of Catalan or Castilian in certain key situations.

*In my own sample of 228 students (see Chap. 5), only 37 percent were native speakers of Catalan, but a total of 58 percent claimed to speak Catalan well or fairly well, and another 30 percent reported that they speak a little Catalan. Only 11 percent of the sample denied any speaking knowledge of Catalan.

This chapter will examine the sociolinguistic basis of this system of ethnic classification. We will then turn to the question of how the system is maintained meaningfully despite widespread bilingualism, and to an examination of the rights and duties of language choice. The norms that govern ingroup communication, the etiquette that dictates appropriate language choice in informal intergroup communication, and the policies mandating language use in formal spheres will be discussed. The final section considers the social meanings attributed to these patterns, particularly their significance for solidarity and power relations in contemporary Barcelona.

Ingroup Language Norms

When individuals are categorized as "Catalan speakers" or "Castilian speakers," the terms usually refer to their native language (**llengua materna**), that is, to the language spoken in the home and learned first during childhood. Some children, however, are raised in bilingual homes (e.g., about 10 percent of the respondents to the experiment discussed in the next chapter claimed to use both languages in the home). Moreover, as we have seen in Chapter 3, people can change their ethnic identity for all practical purposes by acquiring native-like proficiency in the language of the other group. Such proficiency demands not only fluency and phonological accuracy, but knowledge and use of rules for appropriate language choice. The habitual language used in informal interaction within group boundaries (**llengua habitual, llengua de relació**) is as important as native language in determining ethnic identity.

Those who qualify as Catalans not only are raised in Catalan-speaking households but also regularly choose Catalan in informal, noninstitutional interaction with other native speakers of Catalan. A person can become "catalanized" by choosing Catalan as the language habitually and automatically used in informal interaction with Catalan speakers. If a native Castilian speaker adopts Catalan as the regular language of the home and family, that person is for all practical purposes Catalan, and will usually be thought of as such by others. "Simply put, the act of speaking Catalan socially converts an immigrant into a Catalan, whatever her/his origin may be" (Termes 1983: 284).

Castilians, in contrast, are normally those who speak Castilian as a native language and use Castilian with other native speakers of Castilian (as well as in most other situations). However, the regular use of Castilian in informal interaction with native speakers of Castilian does not mean that a Catalan has become "castilianized," as will be seen; only when Catalan speakers regularly choose Castilian in interaction within the Catalan group or introduce Castilian into the home and intimate family circle as a habitual language are they usually considered to be castilianized and no longer truly Catalan.

Thus, as mentioned in Chapter 3, upper-bourgeois families who have shifted to Castilian as a habitual language have forfeited their claim to Catalan identity in the eyes of many Catalans. The norms that govern ingroup language choice are obligatory rules in the sense that when they are consistently violated, the offenders are excluded by definition from the group. Language choice does not simply follow from ethnic identity, but may actually constitute it (cf. Gumperz 1982).

Because of official Francoist language policy as well as the demographic pressure of Castilian-speaking immigrants, for at least the last forty years Catalan has been a minority language in its own territory, in the sense that it has been reserved for private and informal use almost exclusively. Yet it must not be thought that the home has been the only domain where Catalan is appropriate. As both a marker and a reinforcer of ingroup solidarity, the Catalan language signals loyalty to Catalan identity in the face of pressures from the Spanish state and the Castilian-speaking population, and this loyalty has remained a potent force. In addition to the home, friendship networks, voluntary organizations, and even places of business may be identified as Catalan social arenas in which normally only Catalan should be used.

For example, during the first week of my fieldwork, I stopped for lunch in a small town north of Barcelona with a group of Catalan colleagues. Although very Catalanist, they politely used Castilian with me since my command of Catalan was still dubious. As we talked, an apparently regular and eccentric patron of the bar entered and voiced the first rule of ingroup language choice I was to learn: "Why are you speaking Castilian? We're all Catalans here," he shouted. "Stop speaking Castilian." My group sent him on his way, but not before explaining (in Catalan) their violation: "We're *not* all Catalans," they replied. They did not reject the obligation of Catalans to honor their social bond through language choice, but redefined the situation from one of ingroup to intergroup interaction.

Codeswitching in Ingroup Arenas

Though Catalan is the only language generally appropriate for use within Catalan social arenas, conversational codeswitching to Castilian is not unknown. Catalans are accustomed to codeswitch in ethnically mixed groups; there, it is most often the interlocutor's linguistic identity that triggers a switch (as will be discussed in the next section). In such a group, Catalans may alternate languages frequently and rapidly as they direct remarks to Catalans or Castilians (cf. Calsamiglia and Tuson 1980).*

Within Catalan-speaking circles, the topic of conversation does not usually affect language choice. Any topic, from the most intimate to the most formal, can be discussed in Catalan. Speakers do not shift from Catalan to Castilian to mark a change in topic from intimate to formal or a change in the task to be accomplished, as has been reported for many bilingual areas (e.g. Rubin 1968, Blom and Gumperz 1972). Dorian (1981) has found a similar weakness of topic as a code determiner among Scots Gaelic speakers.

Although a formal or technical topic will not cause a speaker to choose Castilian as the vehicle of discourse, it may occasion the use of Castilian loanwords or the ad hoc borrowing of technical terms. For example, a Catalan described the psychological theory he was studying in a Castilian-medium course. His explanation was entirely in Catalan, except for the Castilian terms *alma* (soul) and *cuerpo* (body) to refer to the mind-body distinction of western thought.

---

*It was difficult for me as a non-Catalan to collect reliable data on actual Catalan ingroup language use. Since most Catalans use Castilian when speaking directly to a non-Catalan, my presence in a Catalan-speaking group often triggered switches to Castilian. A flicker of eye contact, a turn of the head toward a non-Catalan like myself, are often enough to trigger a switch to Castilian. Such patterns are misleading when analysis is attempted from audio tapes alone. If anything, then, my account of ingroup Catalan codeswitching is likely to overestimate rather than underestimate instances of switching to Castilian. The generalizations here conform fairly well, however, to those that emerge from fieldwork done by a native Catalan and a bilingual Castilian speaker (Calsamiglia and Tuson 1980).

These borrowings were not caused by a lexical gap in Catalan, but were used in place of ànima and cos. It is possible that they were used because the Catalan contrast set did not evoke all the proper connotations for this speaker. To emphasize the technical sense in which he was using the concepts, he resorted to the Castilian in which they were discussed in the context of his course (much as the English-speaking scholar might use the terms *Gemeinschaft* and *Gesellschaft*, for example).

This kind of usage lies in something of an analytical limbo between lexicalized loanwords, interference, and codeswitching. It can be seen as a restricted kind of metaphorical codeswitching (Blom and Gumperz 1972, Gumperz 1982), in the sense that for the speaker the Castilian terms carry connotations that the Catalan equivalents might not. But this kind of codeswitching is generally restricted to short noun phrases.

Maintaining Catalan as the primary vehicle of conversation, speakers may quote Castilian speakers or cite familiar sayings in Castilian; they may also mimic particular dialects of Castilian for humorous effect.* However, the type of inter- and intrasentential metaphorical codeswitching found among, for example, Spanish speakers in the United States is not common in Barcelona (Poplack 1980, Timm 1975, Zentella 1981). In spite of the association of Castilian with official, public domains and Catalan with informal, ingroup domains, Catalan bilinguals do not often shift to Castilian to evoke connotations of authority, formality, distance, etc. (Gumperz and Hernandez-Chavez 1978). When they switch, the phrase is often marked as borrowed, set off in verbal commas by cues such as pauses or change of pitch and loudness.

It is my contention that because interlocutor identity is a key trigger to codeswitching in Barcelona, this linguistic resource cannot be used routinely to fulfill other functions in ingroup discourse. Extensive use of Castilian in the ingroup could be misinterpreted as a statement about the ethnic identity or loyalty of one of the participants. We have seen in Chapter 3 that Catalan ethnolinguistic credentials

---

*Calsamiglia and Tuson (1980) cite several examples of a Catalan teenager who introduces most of her joking remarks with the phrase *"Dise"* (he/she says, it is said), affecting an Andalusian accent. This is an example of what Giles calls the secondary rather than the primary level of the "accent repertoire," wherein accents are effectively mimicked, but are commonly used only for amusement (1973: 89–90).

can be revoked for significant linguistic behavior that is inconsistent with group membership. Since Catalan is a coveted identity, it is not worthwhile for speakers to risk putting their own or their interlocutor's identity into question by introducing Castilian into their talk. Relatedly, language loyalty and concern about the purity of Catalan run high in some sectors of the Catalan population; introduction of Castilian and Castilianisms is avoided for this reason as well.*

Although codeswitching as a rhetorical device is not widespread among Catalans, some individuals are recognizable as "switchers." (Dorian 1981 similarly reports idiosyncratic switchers for East Sutherland Scots Gaelic.) Even these, however, do not usually rely on the association of Catalan with intimacy and ingroup as opposed to the association of Castilian with formality and public authority to give meaning to their switches. More often, the fact of switching itself is used to mark a statement; the direction of the switch is less important. "Switchers," often socially deracinated, may use the same strategies in intergroup and ingroup communication.

As Gumperz (1982) points out, codeswitching strategies may be used to distinguish new information from old, mark degrees of emphasis or contrastiveness, and distinguish topic from syntactic subject. Codeswitchers can use language alternation to accomplish functions that other speakers signal through syntax or prosody. This is the way in which codeswitching is used by most Catalan switchers; such effects rely only on the juxtaposition of two codes, and not necessarily on the social connotations of either of these codes (cf. Woolard 1987 for an analysis of a Catalan comedian's unusual and successful use of this kind of codeswitching for humorous effect).

As an example of metaphorical codeswitching that draws on associations with the ingroup and the outgroup, Gumperz and Hernandez-Chavez (1978) analyzed a U.S. Hispanic's frequent intrasentential switches between Spanish and English while discussing her attempt to quit smoking. Her many code changes were explained in

---

*Castilian loanwords in Catalan are quite common, both those that fill lexical gaps and those that are "gratuitous" (Mougeon and Beniak 1989). López del Castillo (1976) gives a partial inventory of these. Many Catalans are very sensitive to Castilianisms, and may hypercorrect in compensation. When a choice between two synonyms is available, Catalan purists will often prefer the word that resembles Castilian usage the least; e.g., **ampolla** rather than **botella** for "bottle," since the Castilian form is *botella*.

terms of the contrast between the clinical, detached connotations of English and the personal involvement and intimacy reflected in her use of Spanish. In a strikingly similar situation, a briefer example of Catalan–Castilian codeswitching arose when a Catalan "switcher" discussed how difficult it is to give up smoking. This instance is not amenable to the same kind of analysis, and shows the possible difference between the metaphorical switching of U.S. Hispanics and that which is found in Barcelona. The Catalan speaker said:

[Cat.] **El tercer dia es el pitjor. El primer està bé, perquè ets màrtir. El segon, aguantes perque ho vas fer el primer. Però, el tercer, et dius;** [Cast.] *"No puedo más!! Me da igual!!"*

(The third day is the worst. The first is okay, because you're a martyr. The second day, you bear it because you did it the first day. But the third day you say to yourself, "I can't stand it any more! I don't care!")*

This intrasentential switch cannot be explained on the basis of the personal, intimate connotations of one language as opposed to the formal or detached connotations of the other. In fact, it is in quoting her own hypothetical interior speech that this Catalan speaker resorts to Castilian. The effect attained is both emphatic and humorous, but other Catalan bilinguals agreed that a very similar effect would have been achieved if the switch had taken place in reverse, from Castilian to Catalan. Codeswitching in and of itself is, like changes in rhythm, pitch, and loudness, a device for adding emphasis to an utterance and highlighting significant information. Speakers do not have to rely on the differential connotations of the two languages to achieve this effect, and in Barcelona the strategic uses of such social connotations are in fact highly constrained by the interlocutor principle for code choice.

Intergroup Linguistic Etiquette

Although ethnic-group membership channels social relations and their emotional content, interaction across group boundaries in Barcelona is by no means prohibited or limited to highly restricted domains. Although many Castilian speakers in the suburban enclaves

*This utterance was not tape-recorded, but it was reconstructed and written down within the hour in which it was spoken.

have little opportunity to interact with Catalans, residents of the central urban areas may interact across ethnic boundaries daily. Decisions about intergroup language choices are a constant requirement of urban life. Since language is the primary symbol of group affiliation, the necessity of making language choices can be a constant reminder of ethnic identity and relations.

As a result of the political organization of nationalist sentiment, the conscious organization of language loyalty, and the new political structure of Catalonia, public and intergroup language usage in Barcelona is in a process of change. The outcome of this change is as yet undetermined, and it is seen synchronically as a set of different, often conflicting expectations. It is thus difficult to characterize simply the rules that create expectations about appropriate language use in interethnic situations, much less actual language behavior. Nonetheless, most individuals have a fairly well-developed sense of some language etiquette—that is, notions of when it is correct and polite to use which language—even though these beliefs may enter into conflict with those of other members of the community. This consciousness of etiquette is expressed by informants in spontaneous judgmental comments on interactions, as well as in response to direct questioning in interviews and informal conversation.

Language etiquette serves not only as a basis for choosing among linguistic options, but also as the basis for assigning meaning and motivation to the language choices made by others. I use the term etiquette to stress that choices are made not according to inviolable rules, but rather according to conventions that affect the quality of interaction (Gumperz 1982). Therefore, language etiquette is a concern of both monolingual and bilingual speakers. Though it is the bilingual who carries the burden of making the correct choice, monolinguals also have a well-developed sense of what is right, proper, and polite, and they make judgments about people and their intentions on this basis.

Since virtually all Catalans are known to be proficient bilinguals, it is most often Catalan speakers who must apply the rules of linguistic etiquette. For this reason the discussion of norms of politeness that follows is given mainly from the perspective of the Catalan speaker, focusing on the appropriate choice of Catalan. Still, each norm may be shared by native Castilian speakers and may form the basis of their interpretations of social interaction.

The Accommodation Norm

According to a traditional etiquette dating at least from the Franco years that continues to influence language choices, it is proper to speak Catalan only to those who are known to be Catalan or for whom there are clear signals of Catalan identity, even though it is recognized that most Castilian speakers easily learn to understand Catalan. Catalan is the marked case and Castilian the unmarked case to be used with all unknown quantities as well as known outsiders. By this traditional norm, then, Catalans must accommodate their code to that of their interlocutor. Any sign that an unfamiliar interlocutor may not have fully understood a Catalan statement may provoke a shift to Castilian; the possibility that the addressee may simply not have heard is not considered. (Heller 1982 reports the same phenomenon in Montreal.)

This etiquette of accommodation goes well beyond considerations of comprehension. A very high percentage of Castilians are passive bilinguals (93.5 percent of my experimental sample claimed to understand Catalan at least fairly well); nonetheless, according to the traditional norms, bilingual conversations are avoided. Interchanges in which the participants each use their own language are not considered by traditionalists to be proper, and one language must be elected for the conversation. A person who uses Castilian in response to Catalan, even when giving every indication of perfect understanding, traditionally provokes an automatic shift to Castilian on the part of the Catalan speaker.

The rule for which language to speak in this system is very simple: Catalan should be spoken only between Catalans. In a weak form of the norm, speakers may start out in their own language, then demonstrate accommodation by switching to the interlocutor's if it is different. But in the strong traditional form, a bilingual speaker attempts to diagnose the addressee's language affiliation before speaking, and uses this language.

Though the rule is simple, the difficulty lies in determining how to apply the rule: how do Catalans determine who their co-members of the Catalan linguistic group are? When dealing with an acquaintance or a friend of a friend, the question is settled from background knowledge. But the need to address a stranger is not uncommon in urban life (although it may not be nearly as common as has sometimes been purported). In response to interview questions about what language is used when a conversation must be initiated with a total stranger, I was given four kinds of cues that are used.

First, if the interlocutor initiates conversation, the traditional Catalan takes the language of initiation as an indicator and follows suit, although other criteria discussed below may override this diagnosis later in the conversation. (Recent immigrants are not always fully aware of the ethnic significance of the use of Catalan. It is not uncommon for some of the more adventurous to try out a few phrases, not realizing that they constitute a commitment to converse in the language rather than a symbolic friendly formula.)

Second, I was told that language choice depended on "what part of town you are in." If the location is one considered "Catalan"—an ingroup arena—then an exchange may be initiated in Catalan with a stranger by a "polite" traditional Catalan. "Catalan" identity of location may be attributed to rural areas, to certain neighborhoods of the city itself, and to certain buildings or establishments that are identified with Catalonia—the Generalitat, the Music Palace, and banks, bookstores, restaurants, and other businesses that make explicit their Catalan identity.

The third set of cues are physical and stylistic characteristics of the potential interlocutor. Repeatedly I was told that before speaking, one looks to see if the addressee looks Catalan (**fa cara de català**; literally, "makes the face of a Catalan"). Many informants claim this really means looking at the face—a thin face or a thin nose were cited as characteristic of a Catalan in contrast to most Castilians. In contrast, physical features such as a broad face, darker skin, and stocky build are taken to indicate non-Catalan identity. Other clues include manner of walking or style of dress, although all the styles considered indicative are variations on Western European mass-produced clothing. Most people seem to rely on a physical gestalt, which they admit is not foolproof; one young informant claimed that he could guess linguistic identity correctly from physical appearance about 75 percent of the time.

A fourth cue, used only after conversation has been initiated, is accent and other aspects of speech style. If a Catalan accent is detected in an interlocutor's Castilian, this may induce a Catalan speaker to ask for confirmation of language choice. Sometimes the questions are pointedly about identity—"**Ets català?**" (Are you Catalan?) or "**Ets del país?**" (Are you from [this] country?)—but "**Parles català?**" (Do you speak Catalan?) is also asked.

In turn, grammatical or lexical errors in a learner's Catalan may cause Catalan interlocutors to switch to Castilian. Even the detection of a Castilian accent in otherwise fluent Catalan may trigger a switch to Castilian. If a mistake has been made in choosing Catalan on the basis of any of the above cues, or if in fact any indication is given that the interlocutor does not *speak* (as well as understand) Catalan, the polite traditional speaker immediately switches to Castilian.

Some examples will be given here to illustrate the use of each criterion in the practical application of the accommodation norm.

Interlocutor choice. A particularly striking example of the propensity for a Castilian-speaking interlocutor to cause a switch to Castilian on the part of a Catalan speaker occurred in a public conference on "immigration and national reconstruction." On the day in question, the entire proceedings had been conducted in Catalan. At the end of the formal papers, a member of the audience rose and addressed a question in Castilian to one of the presenters. Clearly the questioner understood Catalan, since he had listened to the talks in this language and formulated his question on that basis. Nonetheless, the presenter who had been questioned responded in Castilian, matching his choice of code to that of his interlocutor in spite of the overwhelmingly Catalan atmosphere and the interlocutor's demonstrated comprehension.

Location. The incident at the small-town bar described under ingroup norms above indicates the power of location to determine language expectations, but it is questionable whether the objector was concerned about "politeness." Another example more clearly demonstrates the importance of location even within traditional etiquette. The distinctly Catalan identity of the Music Palace (Palau de la Música), one of the great and architecturally exuberant symbols of Catalan culture, enabled an usher at a concert to direct me to my seat in Catalan. It became clear that his choice was made within the traditional etiquette rather than on the basis of a more assertive Catalanist norm. Because I did not catch the second part of his instructions, I inclined my head forward, a tacit request for repetition. The usher responded immediately by repeating his instructions in Castilian.

Physical cues. Physical cues can override other cues to appropriate code selection. Even if a location is "very Catalan," a person's appearance may dictate that it is more prudent to initiate an exchange in Castilian. Thus, in a well-known restaurant named after the Catalan flag, the reigning language is clearly Catalan. Upon addressing the waitress for the first time, however, one customer switched from the Catalan he had been using since entering the restaurant. When asked why he addressed her in Castilian, the diner shrugged and said "**No fa cara de catalana**" (She doesn't look Catalan). In fact, it seems that he was correct, and that she was indeed the one non-Catalan worker in the establishment at the time.

There are two important points to notice here. First, there is the low-status occupation of the addressee, which may well have interacted with appearance to suggest a Castilian identity. Informants often discouraged me from attempting to practice my Catalan with waiters, with one telling me that, "unfortunately," most waiters are Castilian speakers (the meaning of "unfortunate" in this statement was never made clear). Although informants never explicitly mentioned class or occupation when asked how they decide what language to use with interlocutors, it clearly is a deciding factor of which many are aware. Second, it is significant in this particular incident that even though the customer might have assumed that the waitress understood Catalan, given the nature and locale of her work, he felt it only appropriate to speak to her in Castilian.

The importance of physical cues in code selection is evident in the behavior of another Catalan informant. Although he claims to be Catalan on both sides of his family as far back as anyone can remember, he is short, stocky, and dark, with a broad nose and wide-set eyes. In short, he looks more like the stereotypical Andalusian than a Catalan. His wife noted, and he acknowledged, that he is often the first to speak in new social situations; he knows from experience that Catalans will assume he is not Catalan and address him in Castilian unless he gives overriding signs of his Catalan identity.

Accent. As we have seen, it is necessary not only that interlocutors understand Catalan in order for it to be traditionally appropriate to address them in Catalan, but also that they speak Catalan. Moreover, for many people, Catalan must be spoken with an identifiably native accent. Such a stipulation reveals the ingroup, boundary-marking nature of this etiquette. For example, Montse is indeed a native speaker of Catalan, but she was raised in a South American

1. A view of Barcelona, city of nearly two million inhabitants, from the port
2. Catalans of all ages perform the national folk dance, *la sardana*

3. Typical panel from a comic book distributed by the Catalan Communist Party (PSUC) to support the 1979 Statute of Autonomy. "With the Statute, who is Catalan? Those who speak Catalan, or will there be two classes of Catalans?" "According to the Statute, there's only one class of Catalans, no matter what language they speak: Catalans are all the citizens who live in Catalonia, who are residents of any municipality of Catalonia. All have the same rights and obligations."

4. Like the PSUC, the Socialist Party of Catalonia (PSC) used the medium of the comic book to campaign for the Statute. The panels on the opposite page are from that publication. Castilian: "Why do they consider themselves a nation?" Catalan: "Between 870 and 878 Guifré el Pilós [was] the first count to receive governing authority from the hands of the Frankish King."

5. "Throughout the 10th and 11th centuries, there were several autonomous counties within 'Old Catalonia.'"

6. "... the Catalan parliament (Corts) was created, supreme consultative and legislative organ of the Principality, which over time would control the royal power."

ART. 1

¿ POR QUÉ SE CONSIDERAN UNA NACIÓN ?

ENTRE EL 870 I EL 878 GUIFRÉ EL PILÓS ÉS EL PRIMER COMTE QUE REP EL GOVERN DE MANS DEL REI FRANC.

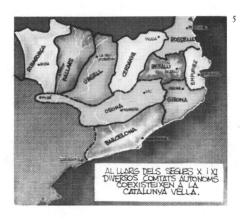

5

AL LLARG DELS SEGLES X I XI DIVERSOS COMTATS AUTÒNOMS COEXISTEIXEN A LA CATALUNYA VELLA.

6

...DURANT EL QUAL FOREN CREADES ES CORTS CATALANES, MÀXIM ÒRGAN CONSULTIU I LEGISLATIU DEL PRINCIPAT, QUE AL LLARG DE LA HISTÒRIA CONTROLARÀ EL PODER REIAL.

7

LLUITEM PER LA NOSTRA GENERALITAT

NO VOLEM UNA GENERALITAT DESCAFEINADA

8

PSA
PARTIDO ANDALUZ

El voto de los Andaluces para el

Partido PSA Andaluz

VOTA L'ESTATUT
25 D'OCTUBRE 1979

GENERALITAT DE CATALUNYA

9

Ciudadanos de Catalunya, lo somos todos.

Claro que alguno puede decir: "Esto no va conmigo". Pero la mayoría —la generalidad— sabe que ser ciudadano de Catalunya no es sólo una cuestión de política. Y desde luego, serlo no significa renunciar a nuestro pasado ni a nuestras tradiciones diversas. Tampoco entraña renuncia o imposición alguna.
Es sentirse ciudadano del lugar donde se nace y donde se hace —o se rehace— la propia vida. Es sentirse ciudadano de donde se tiene el hogar.
Porque ahora, con deberes y con derechos, ciudadanos de Catalunya, lo somos todos.

VOTA

CENTRISTES
DE CATALUNYA (CC-UCD)

Una Catalunya para todos

7. Three campaign stickers from the 1979 referendum on the Statute of Autonomy
8. Electoral campaign advertisement, Andalusian Party (PSA), in *Hoja del Lunes*, March 10, 1980: "The Andalusians' vote for the Andalusian Party."
9. Electoral campaign advertisement, Centrists of Catalonia, in *El Periódico*, Feb. 27, 1980: "We are all citizens of Catalonia."
10. Electoral campaign advertisement, Catalan Communist Party (PSUC), 1980. In this four-page flyer, titled "A Catalonia for All," immigrant Catalonians were pictured in separate panels, along with data on their backgrounds and their statements in support of the party and Catalonia. Left: Rafael Carmona, machinist born in Seville, "Catalan since 1964." His statement read, "The Catalan culture is an open culture in which all the popular accents fit. I'll vote PSUC so that Catalonia will be for everyone." Right: Luis Romero, carpenter born in Cordoba, "Catalan since 1963," who stated, "To vote for PSUC, for a progressive government in Catalonia, . . . means to struggle so that no one ever again has to walk the bitter road of emigration."

11. Some of the apartment blocks for workers that mushroomed in the belt around Barcelona in the 1960's without benefit of urban planning

12. Gaudí's Casa Milà, a prime example of the ornate architecture favored by the urban Catalan bourgeoisie around the turn of the century that graces one of Barcelona's wide central boulevards

country. Her Catalan, though perfectly fluent and idiomatic, shows traces of phonetic influence from South American Spanish (e.g. a dentalized /s/ instead of the almost retroflex /s/ of Catalonia). Montse reported that when she came to Barcelona to attend the university, she had difficulty getting her classmates to respond to her Catalan. Several told her they just could not bring themselves to speak Catalan to her. Similarly, two Catalan-speaking informants from Valencia reported that they often must struggle to get their Catalan interlocutors not to switch to Castilian for them. Many of the characteristic features of Valencian Catalan are similar to Castilian, and these apparent signs of non-native status trigger switches to the outgroup code.

In all of these examples, very subtle cues can provoke a seemingly automatic and unconscious accommodation of Catalan speakers to their supposedly Castilian interlocutors. Not only must both parties to an interchange speak the same language, but if that language is to be Catalan, it often must be believed that both parties are *native speakers* of Catalan. Traditional Catalan etiquette leads speakers to accommodate not simply to their interlocutor's language *proficiency*, but also to his or her underlying *linguistic identity*. Such habits, though based in ideals of "politeness" and almost unconscious, also serve to mark and maintain ethnic boundaries. They virtually preclude the possibility of acquiring Catalan for many Castilian speakers.

Language and Identity: The Ethnographer's Experience

Some of my own experiences best illustrate the extent to which it is considered impolite or inappropriate to speak Catalan to a non-Catalan, even when that person has selected the language herself. As a foreigner not perfectly fluent in either language but exhibiting phonological interference not typical of either group, I often violated expectations, thereby provoking redress or explicit questions regarding language choice that were very useful in revealing underlying norms.

I presented a confusing set of signals when I entered a shop with a bilingual friend with whom I have a predominantly Castilian-language relationship. I addressed the clerk in Catalan and she responded readily in kind. However, when I turned to my companion, we discussed the item I wanted to purchase in audible Castilian, our habitual language. My friend then turned and asked the clerk another question in Catalan. The clerk answered at length in Catalan, then suddenly stopped, looked confusedly from my friend to me, and apologized to me in Castilian. She switched to Castilian for the rest of her response, but our protests finally persuaded her to switch reluctantly back to Catalan. It is important to note that the clerk apologized for speaking Catalan to me, even though I had addressed her in Catalan myself. Her apology seemed as genuine as her confusion, and illustrates the considerations of politeness that may underlie the accommodation norm.

In a similar incident, I accompanied a married couple on a visit to a Catalan-speaking dressmaker. Although I speak Castilian with each member of the couple individually, their own relationship is conducted in Catalan, and we often speak Catalan together when in a Catalan-speaking group. Thus the dressmaker was puzzled by our numerous language switches, although I consistently addressed her directly in Catalan. She switched to Castilian with me when she heard me speaking Castilian to the wife, and was confused by my Catalan responses. Finally, she asked the couple, whom she knew well, "What is she, Catalan or Castilian?" When it was explained that I was a foreigner, a native speaker of neither language, the dressmaker settled into Catalan with me. She commented that she had thought I might be "one of those Castilians who is trying to learn Catalan," and offered this as justification for speaking Castilian to me. Though the dressmaker may have been trying to be polite, her explanation emphasizes the second side of the accommodation norm, that of boundary maintenance.

In both of these instances, my use of Castilian with known Catalan speakers violated ingroup patterns of language choice and revealed that I was not Catalan. In each case, the unfamiliar interlocutor took this violation of ingroup patterns as a cue to speak Castilian to me, outweighing my own intentional signal that I preferred to use Catalan in that interchange.

So thoroughly is the Catalan language identified with membership in the Catalan language group that the Catalan-speaking foreigner is a puzzling anomaly for many traditionalists. When no supporting evidence of my linguistic identity was available, as in the cases above, some of the reactions to my use of Catalan were very telling. For traditionalists, no one but a Catalan speaks Catalan.

Faced with an outsider like myself and no further data or resources for diagnosing my identity, two conclusions were possible: (1) all evidence to the contrary, to conclude that I was not speaking Catalan or could not be spoken to in Catalan, or (2) all evidence to the contrary, to conclude that I was Catalan. One shopkeeper confronted with my foreigner's Catalan and my foreign interactional style decided I must be speaking Castilian. Assisted by my learner's accent, she was able to convince herself that my entire request was in Castilian, but she was unable to account for the one word that had no Castilian cognate, **gos** (dog; Cast. *perro*). "That's Catalan," she said. "Why did you say that word in Catalan?" I pointed out that everything I had said had been in Catalan; after a moment she agreed that indeed it had. A torrent of questioning and comment in Catalan followed.

The second solution to the problem was more common. It is no testimony to my control of the language that when I initiated exchanges in Catalan it was often assumed that I was indeed Catalan; only a Catalan speaker would do such a thing, and only a Catalan speaks Catalan, in the traditional frame. (Americans provoke different reactions than do Castilians who attempt to speak Catalan. Because of phonological similarities between American English and Catalan, we do not exhibit the most typical interference that alerts listeners to non-native status, and are often taken to be speakers of the Mallorcan dialect.) A hotelkeeper was disturbed to hear that I did not have an identity card to give her for my registration; when she found that instead I had an American passport, she was at a loss to understand how I had come by it, since she had been convinced I was Catalan. Again, the mother of one Catalan friend preferred to believe that I was of subnormal intelligence, rather than that I was a non-native speaker of Catalan. After an entire afternoon conversing in Catalan with a family group, it emerged at dinner that I was from California. It took several attempts to convince her that we meant California in the United States. When at last the mother was made to understand, she said, "I thought there was something strange about her. She seemed a little slow to get things and she talks a bit oddly." From that point on she addressed me in Castilian.

The pattern of reserving Catalan for strictly ingroup use, elaborated and generalized during the Franco years, is tenacious and causes great concern to defenders of the Catalan language. However, the picture must not be overdrawn. Use of Catalan is not an embarrassment, and it is not generally considered improper to speak Catalan in front of (rather than directly to) non-Catalans. This contrasts importantly with typical situations such as the Scots Gaelic experience described by Dorian (1981) and the Hungarian community in Austria reported on by Gal (1979), where the minority language was embarrassing or inappropriate in the presence of outsiders.* For example, in six mixed marriages I encountered in Barcelona, the non-Catalan partners found that their in-laws continued to speak Catalan in their presence, although they used Castilian when they addressed the non-Catalan directly. On the eve of the wedding of Puri and Joan, the young Castilian-speaking woman introduced in Chapter 3 and her Catalan fiancé, the groom's mother gave a small party in honor of the bride, attended by female members of the groom's family, several close female neighbors, and me. In spite of the fact that the party was in her honor, all conversation except that addressed directly to the bride was in Catalan. Even her central status did not compel guests to change their normal ingroup language behavior. In more mixed groups, Castilian may normally be the vehicle of general interchange, but Catalans will continue to address each other directly in Catalan with little or no hesitation, even when they are a small minority (cf. Calsamiglia and Tuson 1980).

Variations in the Accommodation Norm

The traditional etiquette is not honored by all, certainly not in the most exclusive form of reserving Catalan only for native speakers that emerges in some of the examples above. Accommodation to an interlocutor's actual language choice rather than underlying linguistic identity is also practiced, and every foreigner who learns Catalan has been gratified by the high praise, flattery, and enthusiastic cooperation this evokes from Catalans who are thrilled that an outsider has taken the time to learn their "small" language. (Most often, however, this flattering response ends in invidious comparisons with Castilians "who have lived in Barcelona most of their lives and haven't learned a word.")

---

*During the years immediately following the Civil War, it was not embarrassing but could often be dangerous to speak Catalan in front of non-Catalans, as Benet (1978) documents.

Even more important, Catalan has political as well as social significance. Its use can express not just the durability of group boundaries, or even simple sympathy with the Catalan nationalist cause, but also rejection of oppression by the centralist state. Although these connotations have long existed, in the 1960's there was a resurgence of the use of Catalan as a symbol of generalized political protest. This political symbolism has led younger, intellectual, and politically progressive sectors of the Castilian-speaking population to accommodate linguistically to Catalans. (As seen in Chap. 3, however, this as often constitutes a move toward identification with Catalan ethnicity as it does the courteous use of Catalan as an intergroup language.)

Such practices still honor the principle of monolingual conversations, but "politeness" no longer necessarily specifies who will accommodate to whom. When two speakers of different linguistic background are both bilingual, the negotiation may involve many steps of accommodation and counteraccommodation (cf. Heller 1982 for a similar process in Montreal). Factors that may influence the outcome include language proficiency, setting, the language of other relationships the interlocutors may hold in common, political commitment, and sheer force of personality. In each case, however, the language choice is individually negotiated. Cultural norms may still give the participants the model of what is desired—a monolingual conversation—but the newly developing etiquette does not specify how this end is to be achieved.

The Bilingual Norm

New sets of expectations that have emerged in recent years are challenging even the monolingual-conversation principle of the traditional etiquette. The "bilingual norm" was espoused by a majority of my teenaged informants, including working-class, monolingual Castilian speakers. If under the accommodation norm it is the addressee's identity that determines language choice, under the bilingual norm it is the speaker's identity that is the principal determinant. According to this norm, it is not impolite for speakers to continue using their own language even when responses come in the other.

Although many informants insisted that this was the norm they believed in, and although it would seem to be one that defines a middle ground of mutual tolerance and respect, this norm is rarely applied effectively. Bilingual conversations in which two participants use different languages are still seen as anomalous and generate unease. They are susceptible to interpretation under the accommodation norm, whereby negative intention can be attributed to the interlocutor. At least one party (usually the Catalan) may be thought rude for refusing to accommodate to the other. A desire to hold the interlocutor at a distance is inferred from the fact that "they care more about their language than about me," as a Castilian informant put it. In their accommodation theory, Giles, Taylor, and Bourhis (1973) have suggested that this interpretation of linguistic accommodation or failure to accommodate is attributable to universal psychological principles, but it undoubtedly derives equally from culture-specific norms and situational standards (Stieblich 1986).

In certain settings, bilingual interchanges can be accomplished successfully. For example, a clearly Catalan bookstore in the center of the city had one elderly Castilian employee who never spoke Catalan. Though Señora Carmen's Castilian did cause more than one customer to falter and eventually switch to Castilian, the expressly Catalan character of the setting and the nature of the business at hand—to locate and purchase Catalan books—enabled firmer souls to speak to her regularly in Catalan.

In my year of fieldwork, however, I witnessed only one stable and solidary bilingual interaction between two people whose relationship was one of friendship rather than business. Two young neighbors whom I had often seen together descended in the elevator with me. They were gossiping, one in Catalan and the other in Castilian, about a fellow they both knew. The girls even referred to him differently in the two languages; to one he was "**Albert**" while to the other he was "*Alberto*." Their conversation continued in this fashion as one accompanied the other to the shop where she worked. This is the only time I saw two apparently friendly people maintain an extended bilingual conversation, without provoking change or intrasentential codeswitching.

Castilian informants who claimed to support the bilingual norm often failed to honor it in practice. Helena, the Catalan-speaking Castilian sketched in Chapter 3, accommodates her husband by adopting Catalan as the language of their relationship; she accommodates friends she has met through him as well. Nonetheless, she insists on her right to speak Castilian in public, using it with Catalan-speaking shopkeepers. If a bilingual conversation results because the shopkeeper is not an accommodator either, she claims this is perfectly acceptable, since she knows that all Catalans understand Castilian.

Yet Helena admits that she can usually pressure an interlocutor to adopt Castilian if she maintains it through a few turns. More important, she says she finds it unbearable when her husband persists in speaking Catalan to shopkeepers who respond in Castilian. Although she may rely on the bilingual norm to justify her own behavior, she cannot accept it from Catalans close to her. Helena's language-specific sense of "fairness" in code choice depends on her association of Catalans with socioeconomic privilege; her view of linguistic etiquette implies a certain noblesse oblige.

Open conflict does not often result from linguistic nonaccommodation; when it does, it is most often in situations of nonsolidary business transactions across not only ethnic but also class boundaries. Although some Castilian informants who worked as service providers insisted that it caused no problems if customers addressed them in Catalan, two incidents illustrate the acrimonious outcomes that can result from nonaccommodation in such situations.

In the first, a group of restaurant customers (all devoted Catalanists) ordered in Catalan, and the waiter repeated each item in Castilian as well as making all further inquiries in Castilian. Although as a newly arrived outsider I naively believed the interchange had gone smoothly, several of the customers did not. After the waiter left, they discussed how offensive and unpleasant his behavior had been, claiming that he had been deliberately hostile to their Catalan. They were angered that one who so clearly understood the language would make no attempt to speak it. When one of the group pointed out that the waiter's resentment was based on his position as a laborer who had been forced to leave his own homeland, another rejected this appeal to a class analysis. He said that he himself would prefer that fate to one of remaining in a homeland that loses its distinctive language and character.

The second incident, in which three Catalan customers interacted with a Castilian waiter, was more explosive. One customer signaled for the waiter in Catalan, "**Escolti**" (Listen; Cast. *Oiga*). The waiter ignored the summons repeatedly, and when he passed nearby, the customer said "**Falta un te amb llet**" (We're missing a tea with milk;

Cast. *Falta un té con leche*). Again the waiter did not respond, and the customer repeated the same phrase loudly and slowly, enunciating precisely. Finally, the waiter asked in Castilian, "*Qué quieren?*" (What do you want?). The customer repeated in Catalan, again getting no response. Her companion launched into a detailed explanation in precise Catalan of the items they had ordered and those they had received, but the waiter did not stay to hear her out. As the waiter stalked away muttering and threw his tray across the bar, the three customers erupted into laughter. I never saw whether they received their tea, but clearly this was not a positive interethnic exchange.

I did once hear a relatively successful conversation among three young women conducted largely according to the bilingual norm. Three university students were chatting on the train about bars and nightspots; two spoke Catalan and one Castilian. One of the Catalans switched languages repeatedly to accommodate her two interlocutors, but the other continued to address both parties in Catalan, while the Castilian responded in her own language. The conversation moved along comfortably, interrupted only by giggles and laughter, and it seemed to me a remarkably successful example of the bilingual norm as practiced by the young. But when the Catalan accommodator got off at an early stop, the pressures for accommodation in a dyadic conversation were apparently too great for the bilingual conversation to be maintained. Without comment, the Catalan speaker immediately switched to Castilian, and the two carried on a monolingual conversation for the rest of their trip. In 1980, the bilingual norm was still not generally accepted and applied in actual interaction, particularly dyadic interaction, in spite of its intellectual appeal to many individuals.

Relations of Power and Solidarity

Considerations of both power and solidarity are intertwined in the interethnic linguistic accommodation pattern. Many Catalans believe that the traditional etiquette is an acknowledgment of the political power of the Castilian language that has been imposed on them. Accommodation of Catalans to Castilian individuals is not just consideration of lesser language proficiency, but a daily deferential bow to the "*lengua del imperio*" (language of the empire). Some Catalans have come to think of even the poorer Castilian-speaking immigrants as informal ambassadors of the Spanish state and resent them as the "fifth column" of the Castilianist linguistic forces. Some few even speak of immigration as a deliberate strategy devised by Franco in the postwar years to undermine the ethnic and linguistic integrity of Catalonia.

If Catalans believe that it is the weight of the empire that makes them accommodate to Castilians, Castilians in turn may express the belief that Catalans who refuse to accommodate linguistically are using nationhood and territorial rights as a means of legitimating the margination of Castilian immigrants in economic, social, and political terms. Their expectation that Catalans should accommodate them by choosing Castilian is not always based on a belief in the overriding privilege bestowed by the Spanish state, although this rationale is frequently invoked. Rather, many base their espoused linguistic etiquette on what they see as the social and economic privileges of Catalans. Catalans are viewed not only as economically privileged, and therefore not entitled to place additional demands on the less privileged, but as (in a perverse way, given political realities) having linguistic advantages. Since it is well known that Catalans *are* bilingual, however unfortunate the reasons, any refusal to accommodate Castilian speakers linguistically may be seen as a deliberate attempt to place them in a position of interpersonal powerlessness. In their own view, Castilian individuals are not responsible for imposing their language on Catalans. They may even agree that it is unjust that Catalans had to learn Castilian, but since they already know it, courtesy demands that they use it. To "impose" Catalan on the Castilian is to flaunt linguistic, social, and economic superiority.

Power is paradoxical, however; other Castilians report that they feel embarrassment when Catalans must demonstrably accommodate to them; it is a sign that they are less cultivated, have less linguistic prowess. The supposed imposition of one's language on others may be taken as an unwelcome claim to power, but the presumption or demonstration of greater multilingual proficiency can also be a display of superiority that discomfits the addressee.

Considerations of social solidarity also create confusion and controversy in decisions about interethnic language choice. According to accommodation theory, linguistic accommodation may seem to be desirable, because likeness signals greater potential for liking; reducing the linguistic distance between two parties reduces social distance. Greater potential for solidary action may seem to be the immediate effect of Catalan accommodation to Castilian speakers. But an ultimate effect of accommodation to Castilians is the denial of access to full membership in the solidary Catalan ethnic group, as many Catalans are quick to point out. Those who cannot penetrate the language barrier cannot penetrate group boundaries; and where group boundaries reflect class divisions, this may be seen as a blockage of upward social mobility. The bilingual faced with a Castilian monolingual is confronted with a quandary. To speak different languages would be to give the appearance of conflict or distance in the immediate interchange; to speak Catalan with those who are less proficient is to force them to demonstrate incompetence and to be in a "one down" position; but to speak Castilian is to exclude the Castilian speaker from the inner circle of the solidary—and economically dominant—Catalan group. It is this paradox that makes it difficult to find happy long-term solutions to the twin problems of language choice and ethnic relations.

Language Use in Formal and Institutional Domains

During the almost forty years of the Franco regime, official policy made Castilian the only language permissible in formal and institutional domains, with few exceptions. Although unevenly enforced, this policy constituted the most thoroughgoing repression suffered by Catalan in its centuries of competition with Castilian. Coinciding with the extension of basic schooling throughout the population, it had profound effects on the linguistic habits of Catalan speakers, making the postwar era the first in which nearly the entire Catalan population is proficient in Castilian. With Castilian legally mandated for formal public use, even when the majority of participants were Catalan, Catalan speakers developed a diglossic linguistic repertoire.

Because this Castilianist norm was largely externally imposed, it has broken down rapidly since Franco's death in 1975. Catalan quickly came to be considered appropriate, at times even obligatory, in public speech for some sectors of the Catalan population.

In spite of a sometimes militant shift to the public use of Catalan, however, language habits in most public spheres—government, media, business—still showed the mark of the Castilianist language policy. One of the principal effects had been to severely restrict literacy

in Catalan. By one estimate, half of the adult Catalan-speaking population used Castilian in personal note-taking (Subirats 1980).
Throughout the city of Barcelona, the majority of advertising in 1980
was in Castilian. The only businesses that had mounted systematic
and noteworthy billboard campaigns in Catalan by this time were
two Catalan banks and, ironically, the multinational Coca-Cola Corporation. Only one daily newspaper of a half dozen in Barcelona was
published in Catalan, and this regularly found itself on the verge of
bankruptcy.

Many people still unreflectingly and automatically considered
Castilian the only appropriate and necessary vehicle of communication in official domains. For example, an ardent Catalan nationalist had difficulty convincing the Catalan employees at her bank that
a letter she needed to present to the national police could and should
be written in Catalan. After consulting the text of the Statute of Autonomy, they finally conceded that it was probably legal. Corresponding with the police in Catalan had been simply unthinkable for
them.

Although the use of Catalan in service-providing businesses was
increasing, much of the private sector was still reluctant to employ it
officially. One Sunday I examined all the help-wanted ads that appeared in the newspaper *La Vanguardia*. A Castilian-language newspaper with a conservative political bent, it is nonetheless the major
vehicle for employment notices in the city. Of approximately 250 positions advertised, only thirteen explicitly required knowledge of
Catalan.* In contrast, thirty-eight specified that knowledge of English was required.

By 1980, official language policy had entered a period of transition marked by ambiguity. The day after the Statute of Autonomy
was passed, a Castilian worker told me that the referendum meant
that everything—radio, television, publications, schooling, cin-
ema—would be in Catalan now: "That's what the Statute says."

Indeed, both the Spanish Constitution of 1978 and the Statute of
Catalan Autonomy of 1979 acknowledge Catalan as an official lan-

---

*Gary McDonogh (pers. comm.) has suggested that the absence of an explicit
requirement of Catalan may mean that it is taken for granted. Though this is possible,
it is unlikely given that the newspaper is published in Castilian, and that current circumstances hardly warrant such an assumption. It is more likely that the absence of
a mention of Catalan indicates either that it is not required or that employers are reluctant to state such a requirement publicly.

guage within Catalonia, but neither specifies what this means. In matters of language, the Constitution (Article 3) states that (1) Castilian is the official language of the state, and all Spaniards have the obligation to know it and the right to use it; (2) the other languages of Spain (*lenguas españolas*) will also be official in the respective Autonomous Communities, in accord with their Statutes; and (3) the richness of the distinctive linguistic modalities is a cultural patrimony that will be the object of special respect and protection.

The Catalan Statute of Autonomy (Article 3) states that (1) Catalan is Catalonia's "own language" (**llengua pròpia**, literally "proper language," in the sense that we use the term "proper name"); (2) Catalan is the official language of Catalonia, as is Castilian, which is official in all of the Spanish state; and (3) the Generalitat guarantees the normal and official use of both languages, will adopt the means necessary to assure that they are known, and will create conditions that will permit them to achieve full equality in respect to the rights and duties of the citizens of Catalonia.

These mandates are vague about the actual roles of each language. No definition of "official language," "own language," "normal use," or "full equality" is given. Though this vagueness allows the Catalan government considerable discretion in formulating and promulgating policy, it also creates tension in the community.

Taken together, the Constitution and the Statute can be interpreted as chartering at least three different arrangements for sharing the official status granted. The Constitution can be read as establishing a kind of territorial-based privilege for Castilian, since it makes knowledge of Castilian obligatory while knowledge of Catalan is not. In contrast, "proper language" in the Statute of Autonomy can be read as giving territorial preeminence to Catalan. And last, the two documents can be read as mandating a scrupulously bilingual policy in which the two languages are fully co-official and therefore, in a sense, not completely autonomous from one another. Wherever one official language is found in public acts or documents, then the other shall also be found.

Given the potential for conflict, it is not surprising that the Generalitat proceeded with relative caution in developing its new linguistic policy. A General Directorship of Linguistic Policy was established in 1980. When I interviewed the general director, she stated that the long-range language-planning goal is to establish Catalan as the territorial and thus sole official language of Catalonia. Nonetheless, her hope was that Catalan would become the normal language of public and intergroup communication through voluntary changes. A decision was made to treat the achievement of the ultimate goal as a process involving several transitional stages, taking place over the span of a generation, and depending primarily on the schools for implementation (cf. Woolard 1986a). One of the first acts of the directorship was a press release commending passive bilingualism as a nondiscriminatory practice and recommending that it be exercised both publicly and privately during a transitional phase in the "normalization" of Catalan (Generalitat de Catalunya 1980). This is an official endorsement of the intergroup bilingual norm, with all its attendant problems, discussed above.

The Francoist linguistic policy could be said to have been based on the motto *"Estamos en España"* (We are in Spain), a clichéd refrain that enrages Catalanists, but that is still repeated on occasion by Castilian speakers. On the other hand, the Catalanist target policy could be said to be based on the theme **"Som una nació"** (We are a nation). Both invoke a territorial principle as the basis for language policy (Ninyoles 1976). The term nation is often used but rarely defined in these debates over language policy; for both supporters and detractors of Catalan nationhood, the term has profound political implications.

The Catalanist goal is almost the mirror image of the traditional Castilianist policy, although there are clear differences in the means advocated to achieve it. Supporters believe that Castilian should be reserved for ingroup use with co-members of the Castilian-speaking community. In all other situations of communication in the larger public or when not all participants are known to be native Castilian speakers, Catalan should be used.

The Generalitat's current policy and long-term goals, though not often articulated explicitly to the general public, provoke complex reactions. On the one hand, some Catalan nationalists feel the government is moving too slowly and believe the long-term goal should be put into practice immediately. They fear that if political expediency and gestures of acceptance toward Castilian speakers prevent Catalan from becoming the primary official language of Catalonia in the very near future, Catalan will die of attrition. The power of Castilian not only locally but as a world language is seen as so great that "equality" before the law is not believed to be sufficient to prevent the ultimate death of Catalan; affirmative action is needed immediately to ensure its survival.

Such nationalists may practice the Catalanist policy of their own accord, and several incidents have provoked public furor. One university professor received intense publicity (and reported threats against his life) when he refused to offer his class in Castilian as well as Catalan. In the newly elected Catalan Parlament, one member absented himself in protest regularly whenever a fellow legislator spoke in Castilian. In another notorious case, a professor was severely criticized for using Castilian in a public forum, although in his speech he defended Catalan linguistic rights. When news accounts alleged that the professor had said he would never speak Catalan, Catalan cultural institutions demanded his resignation.

Many Castilian speakers are in basic sympathy with the long-range linguistic goals of the Generalitat. I was surprised to learn that most of my high school informants in the immigrant suburbs endorsed monolingual Catalan schooling. Even among such supporters, however, there is fear of immediate changes. The same students were quick to say that monolingual Catalan education should begin in the early grades, and it would be unfair to implement it immediately in the higher grades. One university student complained to me that his copy of the entrance examination was printed in Catalan, yet, by his account, he did not complain publicly because he was afraid of being called reactionary or fascist. Pro-Catalan factory workers also considered it unjust and discriminatory that bilingualism was becoming a requirement for some desirable jobs.

These students and workers feared that Castilian speakers in Catalonia would suffer the consequences, and particularly the economic consequences, of a problem that is not of their creation: the barriers to the learning and use of Catalan that existed when they were younger. They are not willing to suffer what they see as retribution for Francoist transgressions, especially when redress of past linguistic injustices implies differential access to economic opportunity.

In contrast, other Castilians object not just to temporary inequities that result from the attempt to put a new policy into practice, but to the long-range Catalanist linguistic goals. Basing their program on the concept of individual language rights as well as the demographic weight of the Castilian-speaking population, they espouse what they view as a truly bilingual public policy. They insist that all government documents should automatically appear in both languages, that schooling at all levels, including university, must be made available in both languages, and that the government must sponsor and fund equally both Catalan- and Castilian-language cultural and artistic projects. Anything less is seen as discrimination against Castilian speakers, and some claim that even voluntary substitutive bilingualism is unjust cultural genocide (Jiménez Losantos 1979). A furor was provoked in early 1981 when 2,300 intellectuals and professionals published a "*Manifiesto*" (Miguel et al. 1981) containing these propositions and protesting perceived discrimination in current policy. Response was quick, and ranged from accusations of demagoguery through suggestions of right-wing conspiracies to relatively dispassionate judgments that total bilingualism on the Brussels model is divisive and unworkable (Pedrolo et al. 1981).

The public battle over Catalan is fought almost entirely on the grounds of power and prestige. The disagreements between those who defend a Catalanist policy and those who defend a bilingual policy stem mainly from different understandings of the balance of power in the contemporary situation resulting from the attention of one group to power in the legal order and the other group to power in the economic order. These in turn are sustained by a difference in historical focus: Catalan defenders emphasize past events and external state-imposed injustices; Castilian-speaking leaders focus on nascent impositions and internal inequalities. Whereas Catalan speakers seek to protect their language from the legal and institutional power of Castilian, Castilian speakers seek to protect themselves from the economic and social power of Catalans. Each interest group at least pays lip service to the respect of the rights and concerns of the other, but each sees the other's assurances as vague and unrealistic rhetoric. The positions taken are further complicated by their deep and long-standing association with larger struggles over political power in the Spanish state.

CHAPTER FIVE ‖‖ THE VALUE OF LANGUAGES

Shared social values or, perhaps more correctly, evaluations, are key links between macrosocial changes and the way people talk. Patterns of language acquisition, of language choice and codeswitching in interaction, and of language shift or change over time often depend on the association of particular language varieties with particular values. The evaluations that have the most critical effects on actual language use are not necessarily the conscious ideological debates discussed in the previous chapter, but rather the automatic associations that are outside of the direct awareness of actors.

The evaluative association that most profoundly affects language choice is that which leads us to believe we are judging not the language, but the person who is speaking. In most people's experience, reactions to certain styles of speech, particularly stigmatized ones, can be visceral, and may conflict with more consciously and deliberately held evaluations of the people we hear. Even in less dramatic moments, we make surprisingly definite judgments about people's intellectual and moral qualities on the basis of the way they "sound" (Allport and Cantril 1934). These associative judgments are part of what Bourdieu (1977) calls our "habitus," in the sense that they are incorporated or literally embodied in our aural perceptions. Though these evaluations derive from the social distribution of language varieties, they become physicalized, naturalized reactions. As such, they can be very powerful determinants of the choices speakers make about acquiring or using particular language varieties. In this chapter we will consider in detail the values that attach to the two languages in Barcelona, not as they are debated publicly but, in as far as ascertainable, as they are felt by people. This less overt phenomenon will be approached using a social-psychological method to complement the observation of behavior and attention to discourse that so far have provided our understanding of the significance of language choice in Barcelona.

The first section of this chapter discusses theoretical problems concerning linguistic prestige or status and solidarity, and sets the questions for our exploration of the value of languages in Barcelona. In the second section, the design and results of a quasi-experimental measure of language attitudes are presented. Throughout that presentation, a very basic explanation of the statistical procedures used is given to guide sociolinguistic readers who might be less familiar with these techniques; forbearance is asked of statistically sophisticated readers. The final section considers the implications of these experimental findings for the evaluation of languages not only in Barcelona but also more globally.

Language Attitudes: Prestige, Status, and Solidarity

Research in several disciplines has pointed repeatedly to two competing social values, or a tension between two distinct poles of evaluation, that organize the social uses of speech. Brown and Gilman's (1960) influential sociolinguistic study of alternation between T-V forms of the second-person pronoun (for example, *tu* and *vous* in French) labeled these two dimensions "power" and "solidarity." In attempts to account for language maintenance and shift, "prestige" is the value that analysts fixed upon earliest and that has been discussed most extensively. Later work on social dialects distinguished an important contrast between "prestige" and "covert prestige," the latter referring to "hidden values" such as toughness or intimacy or loyalty to group (Labov 1966b, Trudgill 1972). This second axis of evaluation has generally come to be referred to as social bonding or group solidarity, a useful shift in terminology, since such values may only be covert in formal and intergroup settings like the interview. Solidarity has been cited in contrast to prestige (or status or power) to account for patterns of codeswitching as well as language maintenance or shift (e.g. Gal 1979, Ryan 1979, Milroy 1980, Dorian 1981).

Correlates to these two dimensions can be found in research done on language and interpersonal relations from a variety of perspectives. Status and solidarity roughly correspond to the psychologists' distinction between "instrumental motivation" (the desire to get ahead in some way) and "integrative motivation" (the desire to be accepted by another group) for second-language learning (Gardner and Lambert 1972). Analogs can also be found in Brown and Levinson's (1978) constructs of "negative face" (the need to be unimpeded) and "positive face" (the need to be accepted) to explain the development of politeness phenomena in linguistic structures. In psychological research on evaluative language in general, Osgood (1964; Osgood, Suci, and Tannenbaum 1957) found three separate underlying semantic dimensions, labeled the Evaluative, Potency, and Activity dimensions. The first two clearly correspond to the two dimensions repeatedly uncovered in research on sociolinguistic values. White (1980) has argued that two dimensions are cognitive universals underlying interpersonal relations and therefore interpersonal language; he has labeled them Dominance and Solidarity.

Although the terminology has fluctuated, the notion of two competing social dimensions of language use has grown more fixed, and has gained wide acceptance in discussions of sociolinguistic phenomena. Identification of those competing solidarity values that might block the effect of status or prestige has been an important tactic in understanding minority-language maintenance in particular. The early generalization that high-prestige languages displace low-prestige languages did not seem to apply to cases like that of Catalonia (Fishman 1964: 55; cf. Weinreich 1974, Ryan 1979). More recent research has tried to confront directly the relation between the two axes of evaluation and their relative influence on the way people talk (e.g. Ryan 1979, Milroy 1980). Nonetheless, as Milroy points out (1980: 195), we do not have a unitary model that accounts for the two opposing ideologies of status and solidarity in an integrated way. One question addressed by the experiment discussed in this chapter, then, is this relationship between the status and solidarity values of Catalan and Castilian.

Refining the theoretical construct of prestige itself has also been a necessary step in improving the power of language values or attitudes to account for linguistic behavior. Weinreich noted that "prestige" had been used to refer to a variety of sources of positive evaluation or esteem for a language, from usefulness to literary and cultural worth, and possibly even emotional significance. He advocated that this ambiguity be resolved by reserving the term prestige for "value of a language for social advance" (1974: 79). Though Weinreich's stipulation of the meaning of prestige has narrowed the field of study, it also has shifted the problem to one of defining "social advance." As Fishman (1964: 54–55) points out, "social advance" is not itself a unitary concept clearly contrasting to ingroup pressures. Fishman was particularly concerned about advance in terms of family and neighborhood standing, and although his point is well taken that this too should be considered "social advance," we might consider these arenas to be captured in the concept of "solidarity." When prestige is contrasted to solidarity, social advance might best be defined as promotion to a status that is consensually validated as higher by the larger social system of which the minority linguistic group in question forms a part.

A lingering problem with the prestige concept is its use to refer to both the social-structural *source* of a language's value and the social-psychological *result* of the situation, i.e. people's attitudes toward the language. Thus value for social advance is assumed to give a language prestige in Webster's dictionary sense: "power to command admiration; ascendancy derived from general admiration; commanding position in men's minds" (Webster 1960: 668). It is this sense of admiration that generally seems to be considered the efficient cause of individual choices in language behavior. However, the explanatory link between social-structural sources of prestige and psychological results is more often assumed than demonstrated. Sociolinguists and sociologists of language focus their research on social-structural variation and its relation to language behavior, whereas "language attitudes" have become a social-psychological field of study. The assumption of a direct link between prestige as social value and prestige as personal attitude is problematic. Even when social advance is defined in the terms of the larger society, at least two distinct sources of linguistic prestige remain, as a Weberian approach to social relations makes clear.

Weber (1958) distinguishes among a social order, economic order, and legal order through which power is allocated, and it is his insistence on this tripartite analytical distinction that is of use to us in thinking about linguistic prestige. Both the economic order and the legal order are the domains of power, or the chance of people to realize their own will even against the resistance of others. The social order is also a vehicle of the distribution of power, but the power it wields is that of honor, also called prestige or esteem. The social order is conditioned by the economic order to a high degree, and in turn reacts upon it, but the two are not identical.

What is of particular importance here is the view of social honor, or prestige, as analytically distinct from, although often intimately intertwined with, the different kinds of power. If we apply Weber's schema to language issues, it becomes clear that we need to measure prestige—social honor, esteem, ascendancy in people's minds—empirically, and not assume it directly from either economic or legal power. Although the distribution of economic and legal power can be fairly easily indexed, the distribution of prestige is more difficult to specify; "methodologically, prestige is almost a residual category" (Hammel 1969: 3). Nonetheless, if we distinguish these three kinds of dominance analytically, we can ask better questions about their relation to language use, maintenance, shift, and change, and quite possibly get better answers.

Giles and Powesland (1975) have correctly noted that there are two kinds of "standard" language varieties. The first is a context standard, a variety associated with official and institutionalized uses; in the terms used here, a context standard is likely to be dominant in the legal order. The second, which Giles and Powesland call a class-based standard, is a language variety associated with a group ranked high in the economic order.

Association with official and institutionalized uses can give a language prestige in two ways. First, upward social and occupational mobility—social advance—often necessitates learning this language to enter and manipulate these formal domains; this is the structural aspect of prestige. Second, from habitual use in these superordinate domains of authority, the language may actually come to "sound" more appropriate to these domains, more intelligent, authoritative, refined, or technical; this is the "attitudinal" aspect of prestige, that which is incorporated into the perceptual disposition of the social actor. When this disposition is created in listeners, an official language has become legitimated, and its authority, correctness, power to convince, and right to be obeyed are generally acknowledged (Bourdieu 1982).

Alternatively, the economic status of a language's speakers has been seen as a prime source of linguistic prestige. Thus, if the speakers of a language generally hold prestigious economic and occupational positions in a multilingual community, the language itself may be prestigious, both necessary for social advance and aurally endowed with authority. What is not often recognized is that this may be the case *even if* that language is *not* commonly used in the superordinate domains of work, government administration, education, or the mass media. As Cooper has noted (1978: 471), the prestige of a language is generally inseparable from the prestige of those who speak it. It is for this reason that Weinreich finds that there is often a corollary to the acquisition of a language for social advance, which is that speakers must learn the valued language well enough to conceal the fact that it was secondarily acquired (1974: 78); they must be able to "pass" as native speakers.

Because the prestige concept has so often gone unexamined, an interesting dichotomy has grown up quietly in sociolinguistic studies. In the literature on intralanguage variation, prestige is discussed most often as deriving primarily from the economic status of its speakers (e.g. Labov 1966a), whereas in work on bilingual and multilingual situations it is frequently treated as deriving principally from functional distribution across domains of use, particularly in education and mass media (e.g. Bourhis 1982). In most situations, there is a high degree of association between the two kinds of power, and most researchers do not consider their relations to language use separately. This may in fact be quite appropriate where access to institutions controlled by the legal order (e.g. schools) is the prime determinant of economic or market situation. The language of the economically dominant group is usually also the language of institutional dominance, the language that receives official support and that is necessary for entry into higher education, government, etc. (Bourdieu and Passeron 1977, Bourdieu 1982).

These relationships among legal or political, economic, and social dominance, however, need to be examined explicitly if we are to build a theory that models the way prestige passes from the social structure to the individual's mind and mouth, and thus adequately accounts for language choice, maintenance, and shift. Such a research agenda has practical implications as well: those who wish to influence the position and use of particular language varieties need to understand the relative effects of intervention in legal and economic spheres.

Linguistic Prestige in Catalonia

The Catalan case offers an unusual opportunity for the examination of these relationships among spheres of dominance. In Catalonia, power in the economic order and power in the political order, though not completely unrelated, are distinct in their historical development and modern distribution. Moreover, one language, Castilian, has been associated with political dominance and has long enjoyed exclusive institutional support, whereas the other, Catalan, is associated with the economically dominant group in Catalonia.*

Within the legal or political sphere, it was of course during the Franco regime that the Castilian language held greatest sway. By 1980, when the following experiment was carried out, more liberal linguistic policies were formally entering into effect. Nonetheless, change came slowly, and Castilian was still overwhelmingly the dominant language in most institutions, especially the public schools and information media. Although one radio station broadcast its entire programming in Catalan, the state-controlled television provided only twenty hours of Catalan programming a week in 1980, in contrast to 150 hours in Castilian (Consell Executiu de la Generalitat de Catalunya 1981: 20).

By the 1979–80 school year, the only requirement for Catalan was that it be taught three hours per week; even this was not met everywhere because of a lack of trained teachers. Only 4 percent of the schools in Catalonia taught entirely in Catalan (ibid.). It was not until after the 1979–80 school year that teaching in Catalan began to increase progressively (Arnau and Boada 1986: 113). Castilian

---

*Catalan is dominant in the economic order in the sense that it is the native language associated with those who dominate in the marketplace. The Catalan language itself is not necessarily the language of economic exchange. The social concomitants of a language's value in the economic order in this strict sense could better be studied in societies where the dominant language of the marketplace differs from that of legal institutions; such circumstances are more frequent in the plural societies of the Middle East, Asia, and Africa.

was still the hegemonic language in official institutions, particularly those that touched the lives of young people.

Although in the political order Castilian was associated with dominance, within the economic order of Barcelona that language is strongly associated with the working class, and particularly the unskilled sectors where southern immigrants and their offspring are concentrated. The higher one moves on the economic scale, the more frequently Catalan is likely to be the spoken language (except at the highest peak of the bourgeoisie, where Castilian would be heard) (Giner 1984: 48). The models of economic success in the public consciousness—the factory owners, managers, engineers, doctors, lawyers with whom the immigrant population may come in contact—are a predominantly Catalan-speaking as well as Catalan-origin group (ibid.). This is reflected in one Castilian teenager's explanation of why more Catalan speakers are found in academic high schools and Castilian speakers in technical high schools: "Catalan people, the parents, are accustomed to think that their son will be a lawyer, their son will be an architect—things like that. It's logical. Just having more money; the parents, for example, have a factory or something, you know? Here in Catalonia you see more rich people who are Catalan than who aren't."

Given the conflict between the economic and the official, institutional sources of linguistic power in Catalonia, the relative prestige of the two languages in the sense of "ascendancy in people's minds" (i.e. attitudes) is not a foregone conclusion. Both languages have "value for social advancement," depending on how such advancement is conceived.

A Formal Measure of Language Attitudes

To explore the values of Catalan and Castilian, a quasi-experimental measure of language attitudes known as the "matched-guise" test was used.* The original matched-guise test was designed by Wallace Lambert and colleagues over twenty years ago to study

---

*The design is quasi-experimental rather than experimental, as is most work in the social sciences, because subjects are not randomly assigned to groups. Rather, the groups—in this case, Catalan and Castilian—are to be discovered in society and are not manipulable by the experimenter. This means that correlations that are discovered may be spurious; we cannot be certain that we have focused on the aspect of the social situation that truly explains the effect observed.

the social-psychological effects of the bilingual situation in Montreal (Lambert, Hodgson, et al. 1960). Similar designs have since been used to investigate language attitudes in various regions of the world, in situations of dialect variation as well as bilingualism (e.g. Giles 1970, Wolck 1973, Bourhis, Giles, and Lambert 1975, Tucker and Lambert 1969, El-Dash and Tucker 1975, Ryan and Carranza 1977).

In the matched-guise test, listeners are asked to evaluate the personal qualities of tape-recorded speakers using the languages in question. Each speaker on the tape reads the same prepared text once in each language, but listeners are not told of this in advance (and usually do not notice the repetition of speakers). By holding context, text, and speaker constant and varying only the language used, the test allows us to capture the effect of language choice on the impression a speaker makes.

In his early study, Lambert hypothesized that in a bilingual situation, listeners should respond more positively to the use of their own native or habitual language than to the outgroup language. He was therefore not surprised to discover that Montreal anglophones reacted more positively to a balanced bilingual when he used English rather than French in controlled experimental conditions. More surprising at the time was the discovery that francophones also reacted more positively to the use of English than French, and were in fact more extreme in their reaction than anglophones. The results were interpreted as a measure of the lack of social prestige for the French language and of the self-stigmatization of francophones in Canada.

Similar results and similar interpretations have come out of most later studies of minority linguistic groups using this technique, although variations and refinements in the experimental design make them not entirely comparable. In accord with the work on status and solidarity discussed above, later studies have often found that attitudes toward languages vary on two distinct dimensions. Although in general the use of nonstandard and minority languages causes speakers to be downgraded in terms of competence, status, and other dominance factors, they are often found to be more highly valued on such "affective" traits as attractiveness, persuasiveness, integrity, toughness, etc. (Wolck 1973, Giles 1973, d'Anglejan and Tucker 1973).

Within the framework of the matched-guise test, Carranza and Ryan (1975) formalized the distinction between the dimensions of status and solidarity. In their investigation of attitudes toward Mexican-American speech, they used factor-analytic methods to confirm the distinctive patterning of status-stressing traits and solidarity-stressing traits in the evaluation of speakers. In this sense, the present study used a design more similar to that of Ryan and Carranza than to that of the original Lambert study. On the basis of the theory emergent in the cumulative work done from a variety of perspectives, separate questions about status and solidarity in language attitudes guided the experiment.

In the realm of status, two different hypotheses about the relative worth of Catalan and Castilian could be proposed. If the legal order and institutional support are the primary sources of language status, we would expect Castilian to be more highly valued. Many Catalanist commentators have adopted this position, attaching prestige value to schooling and mass media especially, and assuming that these factors greatly influence the population's attitudes toward the two languages (e.g. Strubell i Trueta 1981a, Argente 1980).* Those outside investigators who have included Catalonia in their general statements about language prestige have based their characterization on this same position (Ryan 1979, Milroy 1980, Fishman 1964). In contrast, if language status originates most importantly in the class position of its speakers, or their power in the economic order, then Catalan would be valued more highly than Castilian.

In considering the solidarity dimension of language attitudes, we are led to a different set of expectations about the relative response to the two languages. In most studies, it has been hypothesized that social solidarity should lead individuals to rank their own native language highly in certain aspects, even when they have downgraded it in terms of status or prestige, although this hypothesis has not always been confirmed (Carranza and Ryan 1975). I have claimed in Chapters 3 and 4 that language choice is critical in the definition and maintenance of group boundaries in Barcelona. If this is indeed the case, individuals should attribute greater solidarity value to their own lan-

---

*Although most Catalan commentators attribute greater prestige to Castilian on the basis of its institutional dominance, the class connotations of the language have by no means gone unnoticed (Arnau 1980, Esteva Fabregat 1974, 1978, Strubell i Trueta 1978). In a public conference on nationalism and immigration in 1979, the Catalan sociolinguist Francesc Vallverdú specifically noted that it is not television and other mass media that give a language prestige, but the class position of its speakers.

guage, regardless of the relative prestige of the two languages. When judging affective characteristics of speakers, Catalans and Castilians should be expected to react differently rather than to share a normative standard.

The Experiment

In the spring of 1980, I conducted a matched-guise test with 240 high school and college students in classrooms of five schools in the city and suburbs of Barcelona. The student respondents (who will sometimes be referred to as Rs) were asked to listen to a tape recording of ten female voices reading the same passage in Catalan and Castilian and to rate the speakers on fifteen personal traits on an accompanying questionnaire. Respondents were unaware that only five speakers were heard, each reading the text once in Catalan and once in Castilian.

The Text. The passage used in the experiment was selected according to three criteria: appropriateness to the school domain; absence of specific association with either Catalan or Castilian culture (Iberian literature, politics, history, family life, etc., were topics excluded for this reason); and ease of achieving comparability in the two versions. The text finally chosen, taken from a high school reader, gave a short explanation of the logic of Euclidean geometry, comparing it to the branching of a tree. An earlier attempt to translate a livelier passage revealed that adjectives and other qualifiers—vivid language in general—were the most troublesome for achieving equivalence of register and tone in translation. For this reason, a rather dry academic passage was finally selected.

Although other investigators who have employed the matched-guise method have not discussed the means by which they ensured that the two texts used were semantically and rhetorically equivalent, it is quite important that the two versions of the text be matched not only for referential meaning but for style as well (unless, of course, style is the subject of investigation). If the text is more colloquial, informal, colorful, or modern in one language than in the other, for example, this will undoubtedly affect the personality judgments offered by bilinguals. For this experiment, the text was translated into Catalan from the original Castilian by a native linguist, then back-translated by a second linguist to identify any points where the two texts were not maximally equivalent. It was this process that led to the discarding of the first text. The back-translation of the text on Euclid differed from the original Castilian only in two verb forms, two word placements, and six lexical choices. These were considered insignificant differences by the translators, and after minor adjustments we concluded that the two versions were as unambiguously equivalent in tone and meaning as could be hoped. The final text consisted of two paragraphs that took approximately a minute and a half to read aloud (see Appendix B).

As a rather formal and scholarly piece, the text was intended to be appropriate to the school setting. This created a possible bias against Catalan, given the recent history of its use and the fact that two-thirds of the Rs attended Castilian-language schools. The question of which language to use in the classroom, however, was an urgent practical issue, and it was useful to capture contemporary student reactions to the use of Catalan for scholarly purposes.

The Speakers. No attempt was made to approximate some ideal of the perfect bilingual in the choice of speakers, although this was done in Lambert's original work. Rather, the concern of the experiment was to reflect more accurately the consequences of actual language choice in Barcelona. Speakers who do not betray their linguistic origins in their pronunciation of one or both languages are rare in Barcelona (and, one suspects, elsewhere). We have seen in Chapter 4, in fact, that accent is often used to diagnose ethnic identity. Therefore, speakers were carefully recruited to represent in so far as possible the actual spectrum of accents in Barcelona. A more realistic evaluation of the social consequences of language choices actually available to real speakers could be achieved by making use of typical accents than by trying to represent an ideal bilingual.

All speakers selected were female teachers in their twenties or thirties. The use of female voices is particularly appropriate in the school setting since, in Barcelona as in the United States, a high proportion of teachers are women.* The first speaker was included only to familiarize Rs with the test procedure by providing a trial run; her results will not be considered here. Of the remaining four, two are Castilian-dominant and two are Catalan-dominant. The numbers

*It would of course be of interest to compare reactions to male speakers, but difficulties in preparing test materials in the field with limited equipment prevented this.

assigned to them in this discussion reflect their position on a range from less to more markedly Catalan, rather than the actual order of presentation on the tape.

Speaker 1, Angeles, is Andalusian and has lived in Barcelona only two years. Her Castilian is strongly marked by an Andalusian (Seville) accent, and her Catalan is highly marked as non-native, although she reads fluently.

Speaker 2, Dolores, was evaluated by language teachers who served as independent judges as speaking a very standard, very "good" Castilian with none of the Catalan phonetic interference frequently found in Barcelona Castilian. As a native of Barcelona and a speaker of Catalan since age thirteen, she was not readily identifiable by these judges as either a native or non-native when she spoke Catalan, although she shows a fair amount of phonetic interference from Castilian, especially in vowels and some voiced fricatives and affricates.

Speaker 3, Montse, is a native bilingual of mixed parentage who uses Catalan as her primary and habitual language and has a very strong Catalan identity. A certain amount of Catalan phonetic interference can be heard in her Castilian, especially in the vowels and the velarized /l/; such interference is typical of the Castilian spoken by natives of Barcelona. Her Catalan was judged to be recognizably "good" Barcelona Catalan, which has come to be a virtual standard for Catalan speakers.

Speaker 4, Núria, was the only nonresident of Barcelona, and she represents the extreme "Catalan" end of the spectrum. As a native and resident of a provincial city, she speaks a Castilian clearly recognizable to the judges as that of a Catalan, and her accent in Catalan is "dyed in the wool" (de la ceba, translated freely), more characteristic of the small provincial city than of Barcelona.

Each speaker was taped several times to eliminate hesitations and reading mistakes, but no attempt was made to correct pronunciation, since these speakers were chosen precisely to represent different accents. This strategy was apparently effective, since several respondents commented that the voices were all very "normal" and reminded them of people they knew; one complained that they were "too normal" to be interesting. In the final tape, the voices were reordered so that the two versions of a single speaker would be maximally separated. A silence of one and a half minutes was inserted after each voice to allow the Rs time to complete each evaluation before going on to the next.

The Questionnaire. The respondents were given a bilingual set of response sheets and were free to choose the language with which they were more comfortable. For each of the voices there was a separate sheet with an identical set of questions. Respondents were asked to rate each voice on each of fifteen traits on a six-point scale ranging from "Very little" to "Very much" (see Appendix C). The framing question was: "Does the person who is speaking seem to you to (be/have) . . . ?" The traits were the following:

1. Intelligent
2. Likeable
3. Cultured
4. Physically attractive
5. Trustworthy
6. Sense of humor
7. Ambitious
8. Open
9. Self-confident
10. Progressive
11. Generous
12. Leadership ability
13. Amusing
14. Hardworking
15. Proud

An attempt was made to base the list of traits on natively important concepts, so that respondents would not be forced to make judgments that they would not normally make about people. Most of the traits were taken from descriptions given in earlier interviews and conversations in Barcelona, and the list was constructed with the assistance of native informants.* The traits were also selected because intuitively they seemed to represent the status and solidarity dimensions of evaluation. The two types of traits were scrambled so that they did not cluster in the questionnaire. The final sheet of the questionnaire asked for personal data on family background, language use, etc., from each respondent.

---

*The English translations of some of the traits are rather loose. *Culta*, for example, is a frequent descriptor in Barcelona, and it implies education, good upbringing, and good taste. Lack of **cultura**, however, can mean not simply vulgarity or lack of training in the finer points of high culture, but illiteracy and even bad hygiene. Two traits reflect the interests of the researcher more than the usual mode of evaluation in the community and thus are probably less appropriate measures. They are "self-confident," which was clearly meaningful to the Rs but is not a common descriptor, and "leadership ability," which caused some problems because it can be taken in an almost strictly political sense. However, attempts were made to minimize this problem through classroom discussion, and the method of data analysis also minimizes the importance of these less than perfectly appropriate traits.

The Respondents. There were several reasons for choosing to perform the test in schools. A major one was of course convenience. I was provided access to schools by acquaintances who were teachers; school populations are preselected for age; the type and location of the schools served as a quite accurate index to the representation of social classes and ethnic groups in the sample; and many respondents could be tested at the same time. Moreover, this kind of activity is already considered socially appropriate and meaningful in classrooms. Respondents were able to make sense of the experiment as an event and respond with less difficulty than might occur in other settings.

Two other considerations make the choice of the school setting meaningful as well as expedient. First, as mentioned above, an immediate concern of Catalan language planners is the implementation of Catalan in the classroom. I could arrive at conclusions most applicable to this concern by investigating within the classroom. Second, it is this younger generation whose reactions to the language problem will determine the direction that changes take in the near future. The school-aged population is of critical importance in a study of language attitudes in a shifting social and political situation.

The particular schools were chosen in an attempt to represent most of the social strata of the Barcelona area except the most elite. The first school was a teacher-training college where Catalan was the dominant language, both in instruction and in informal interaction. The students, however, were of both Catalan and Castilian origin, and most of them were from working-class and lower-middle-class (**menestralia**) backgrounds. Two private academic high schools (**instituts de batxillerat**) in Barcelona were also chosen. The first was relatively expensive and drew its students principally from the bourgeoisie; most of the respondents' parents were managers or owners of business enterprises. Catalan had recently become the language of instruction in this school, although a surprising number of the students came from bilingual or Castilian-speaking homes.*

The second private school was more modest, drawing its students from the lower bourgeoisie and **menestralia** of the center of the city; most of the parents were shop owners, middle- or low-level man-

---

*It is unfortunately unclear whether these upper-middle-class Castilian-speaking families are "renegade Catalans" now turning back to the Catalan language, or Castilians by origin; almost all of the parents were born in the Barcelona area.

agers, and other white-collar workers. These students were of both Castilian and Catalan origin, about equally mixed, and the directors of the school were Catalan. Castilian was the dominant language of instruction, but teachers often spoke Catalan to students in informal interaction even within the classroom.

The fourth school was a small, relatively new academic-track public high school serving the immigrant neighborhoods of a working-class town on the urban periphery. The language of instruction here was primarily Castilian. The students were overwhelmingly working-class Castilian speakers, although Catalans were sprinkled among them. The fifth and last school was also a public high school in a peripheral working-class area, but offered vocational training (**formació professional**). Again Castilian was the dominant language of instruction, but Catalans from the old core of this peripheral city were better represented among their immigrant-origin classmates, in training for some of the more desirable skilled occupations.

Although 240 students participated in the experiment, several questionnaires were excluded for various reasons, and the final sample consisted of 228 respondents.* The ages of the final sample ranged from fourteen to twenty-nine years, and the median age was seventeen. Of the 228 respondents, 117 (51 percent) were male and 107 (47 percent) were female (4 Rs neglected to indicate their gender). Males predominated slightly among Catalan speakers, but the sexes were equally represented among the Castilians.

Of the original 240 respondents, well over half reported that they speak only Castilian in the home, approximately one-third reported that they use only Catalan, and a little less than 10 percent reported themselves bilingual speakers in the home. A very small number claimed to be home speakers of another Iberian or foreign language, either alone or in combination with Castilian (Fig. 5.1). The bilingual and other-language groups could not be considered separately in the analysis because of their small size. Therefore, the personal data sheets were reexamined for further information. If it could be determined from the reports on the parents' language in the home that one

---

*One college student over forty years old was eliminated, to keep the sample within a reasonable age span. Three Rs were excluded because they had seen through the experiment and realized there were only five speakers; though they claimed they had not let this affect their response, their tests were eliminated as possibly invalid. Only one case had to be excluded because the questionnaire was improperly filled out.

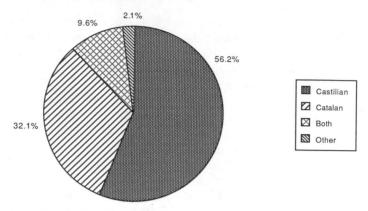

Fig. 5.1. Respondent's home language, original sample (N = 240)

language was dominant, the self-reported home bilinguals were reassigned to that group; others were excluded from the analysis.* In the final "clean" sample of 228 Rs (the basis for all further discussion), slightly less than two-thirds were classed as Castilian speakers and more than one-third were Catalans (Fig. 5.2). Though the sample is clearly weighted toward Castilian speakers, it accurately reflects the linguistic makeup of the student population in the Barcelona area. Arnau (1980) estimates that only about 34 percent of primary school students are Catalan speakers.

Just under half of the respondents said that they use only Castilian with friends, 42 percent reported that they use both languages, and fewer than 10 percent said they speak only Catalan with friends (Fig. 5.3). This means that approximately three-fourths of the Catalans now use Castilian with some of their friends, whereas only about one-fourth of the Castilian speakers have learned to use Catalan in friendly exchanges.† Although self-report is not particularly reliable,

---

*Of the original 240 Rs, 23 reported themselves as bilingual in the home. On the basis of parental language use, six were recoded as Castilian and nine as Catalan. The eight remaining "true" home bilinguals were not included in further analyses. (One of these was eliminated in any case for other reasons, given above.) Of the five Rs who reported themselves speakers of another language, four were recoded as Castilian and one as Catalan on the basis of reported parental language use.

†These figures are slightly skewed by the fact that a few home bilinguals were coded into a monolingual category for the purpose of analysis, but the general pattern still holds.

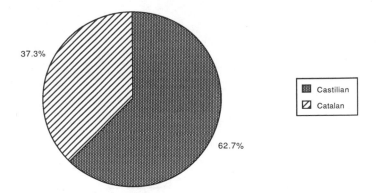

Fig. 5.2. Respondent's home language, final sample (N = 228). Figs. 5.3–5.7 are based on this sample.

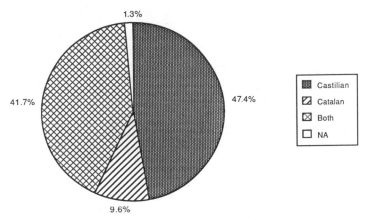

Fig. 5.3. Language used by respondents with friends

these figures present a reasonably likely linguistic population, given the predominating language habits reported in Chapter 4.

Three-fourths of the respondents claimed to understand Catalan well, and no one claimed not to understand it at all (Fig. 5.4). But when questioned about speaking ability, under one-half reported speaking Catalan well, and almost the same number claimed to speak it only a little or not at all (Fig. 5.5). Taken together, these figures accurately reflect the high degree of passive bilingualism in Bar-

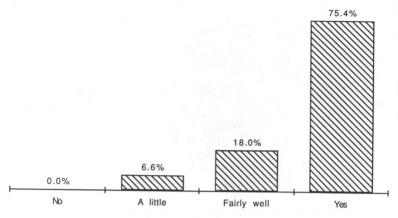

Fig. 5.4. Do respondents understand Catalan?

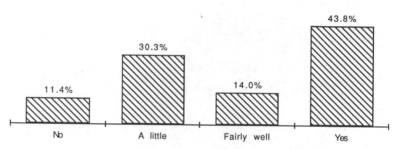

Fig. 5.5. Do respondents speak Catalan?

celona. (Rs were asked about reading and writing ability as well; see Figs. 5.6 and 5.7.)*

Over three-fourths of the respondents were born in Catalonia; Andalusia was the second most frequent place of origin with 9 percent (see Table 5.1). However, fewer than half of the respondents' parents were born in Catalonia, and approximately one-fourth of the parents were from Andalusia (see Table 5.2). Thus only about one-

---

*In reporting whether they speak, understand, read, and write Catalan, the highest choice respondents were given was "yes," rather than "very well," or some other evaluative formulation. Even many native, habitual Catalan speakers in the Barcelona area are insecure about the quality of their Catalan, believing it to be heavily influenced by Castilian, and are unlikely to make such a positive claim as "very well." A tendency to underreport proficiency because of linguistic insecurity often characterizes minority-language communities.

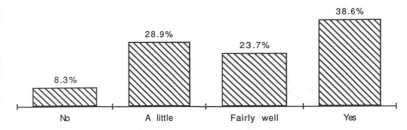

Fig. 5.6. Do respondents read Catalan?

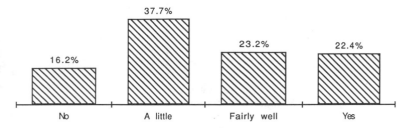

Fig. 5.7. Do respondents write Catalan?

third of the Castilian speakers in the sample are first-generation immigrants. The remaining two-thirds were born in Catalonia of
Castilian-speaking families. From another perspective, these figures
show that fewer than half of those respondents born in Catalonia are
native Catalan speakers. Again, this seems to accurately reflect the
linguistic profile of the Barcelona area.

Administration of the Test. I was introduced into each school by
friends or acquaintances who were teachers, and their assistance ensured a cordial, interested, and helpful reception for me. In all but
one case, I visited the school, met with staff, and discussed the student population, language issues in the school, and the details of the
experiment with the staff before the day of the experiment. Permis-
sion was obtained from teachers and principals in advance, and from
students before the test. The experiment was carried out in classrooms during classtime, with the consent and cooperation of all participants. I gave the instructions, usually with the assistance of the
teacher, in the language of the classroom: Catalan in two cases, Castilian in two cases, and both languages in one case.

TABLE 5.1
Respondent's Birthplace
(N = 228)

Place of birth	Number of respondents	Percent of total
Catalan-speaking areas	182	79.9%
Barcelona	170	74.6
Other Catalan provinces	8	3.5
Balearics and Valencia	4	1.8
Andalusia	21	9.2
Extremadura	5	2.2
Murcia	3	1.3
Aragon	4	1.7
Castile (Old and New)	7	3.1
Euskadi	1	0.4
Galicia	1	0.4
Foreign-born	4	1.8

TABLE 5.2
Birthplace of Respondent's Parents
(N – 228)

Place of birth	Respondent's mother		Respondent's father	
	Number of respondents	Percent of total	Number of respondents	Percent of total
Catalan-speaking areas	106	46.5%	100	43.8%
Barcelona	80	35.1	78	34.2
Other Catalan provinces	19	8.3	19	8.3
Balearics and Valencia	7	3.1	3	1.3
Andalusia	57	25.0	52	22.8
Extremadura	11	4.8	14	6.1
Murcia	12	5.3	16	7.0
Aragon	12	5.3	16	7.0
Castile (Old and New)	16	7.0	18	7.9
Euskadi	1	0.4	2	0.9
Galicia	5	2.2	2	0.9
Asturias	1	0.4	—	—
Foreign-born	4	1.8	3	1.3
NA	3	1.3	5	2.2

The experiment was introduced following Lambert's model: respondents were told that the test was designed to explore the extent to which a person's voice determined other people's expectations of him or her, and they were reminded of the way in which we form an image of a person just from talking on the phone or listening to the radio. They were *not* told that they would hear the same person more than once, or that the languages themselves were the subject of investigation.*

The students were encouraged to ask questions if they had any difficulties completing the task, and were assured they would not be tested on the content of the passage. Response sheets could be filled out while the person was talking, and an additional minute and a half was given between voices to complete each sheet. Most Rs began to respond quickly, and few had any difficulty completing the task in the time allotted after the first trial run. Somewhat to my surprise, most of the students approached the task earnestly and patiently.

Analysis of the Data

In analyzing the data, two basic strategies were possible. One was to examine the judgments on each of the fifteen traits separately, as was done by the Lambert team in the original matched-guise study. Alternatively, the set of personality descriptors could be explored statistically to confirm whether they showed internal structure along the two dimensions for which they had been selected intuitively. Reduction of the data to the principal components of this structure would both minimize the unwieldiness of the data and provide greater coherence in the interpretation of the results. Though the first option was chosen in the initial exploration of the data through the paired *t*-test statistic (Woolard 1984), the second approach was used in the final analysis of variance that will be reported here.

Principal Component Analysis. To determine the extent to which the two underlying semantic dimensions had indeed been captured in this test, the intercorrelations among the fifteen traits were subjected to a type of factor analysis known as principal component

---

*When informed after the experiment about the "trick" in the design, most Rs found it very hard to believe that they had heard each speaker twice, although a few did say that they had suspected they heard one or two of the voices more than once. Three cases were removed from the sample because these Rs recognized the voice of a speaker who was coincidentally a former teacher of theirs, and one other boy guessed with some certainty that he had heard only five speakers. When asked whether this insight had affected his responses in any way, the student's frank answer was almost as revealing as the experiment itself: "No, I know I gave them different scores because I felt differently about them in the two languages." (Nonetheless, his questionnaire was eliminated from the final sample.)

analysis.* The objective of factor analysis is to represent a set of variables in terms of a smaller number of hypothetical variables (Kim and Mueller 1978). The pattern of relationships among the variables is used to reduce the original data set to scores on a smaller set of components. As a simple example, if high scores on Trait 1 are generally associated with high scores on Trait 2 and Trait 5, we might hypothesize that there is some single source variable that creates this relationship among them and "extract" this variable from the data.†

In this analysis, three components were found to have eigenvalues greater than 1, meaning that they account for at least as much of the total variance as did any of the original traits. Together, these three principal components accounted for almost 62 percent of the total variance in the data set, as shown below. Only these three components were retained for further analysis.

Component	Eigenvalue	Percent of variance
1	5.45	36.3%
2	2.61	17.4
3	1.18	7.9

There are many mathematically equivalent ways to define the underlying dimensions of the same data set, and the solution obtained in the initial extraction is not necessarily the simplest to interpret. Therefore, the solution was rotated (using the Varimax method) so that in the final solution each of the original fifteen traits is best accounted for, or loads highly on, only one of the three principal components. This procedure makes the semantic content of the components more transparent while preserving their independence from one another.

Table 5.3 presents the three principal components identified. The original traits are listed, along with their factor coefficients on each component. For ease of interpretation, the trait is printed in boldface under the component on which it had the highest loading. It is ap-

*The factor analysis subprogram PA1 of SPSS (Nie et al. 1975) was used. There were some missing cases, and pairwise deletion of data was used.

†In addition to reducing the number of variables to be discussed, the principal-components strategy has the advantage of transforming the data from an ordinal scale of measurement to a continuous scale. Ordinal data are not, strictly speaking, appropriate measures to be subjected to analysis of variance (or its simple form, the t-test), whereas the standardized scores that can be generated from principal component analysis are.

TABLE 5.3
Varimax Rotated Factor Matrix

	Factor		
Trait	1	2	3
1. Intelligent	.17	.80	.10
2. Likeable	.81	.19	-.02
3. Cultured	.13	.84	.11
4. Physically attractive	.60	.24	-.02
5. Trustworthy	.51	.41	-.33
6. Sense of humor	.85	.07	-.01
7. Ambitious	.02	.29	.77
8. Open	.77	.23	.03
9. Self-confident	.24	.68	.30
10. Progressive	.34	.47	.15
11. Generous	.58	.19	-.46
12. Leadership ability	.15	.74	.24
13. Amusing	.86	.09	.00
14. Hardworking	.11	.67	-.13
15. Proud	-.07	.16	.82

parent that the three components are very similar to those found by Osgood (1964; Osgood, Suci, and Tannenbaum 1957). Examining Table 5.3, we can see that Factor 1 stresses affective characteristics (Osgood's Evaluation). Such qualities as likeability, trustworthiness, humor, and openness are those that have been seen to be stressed in relations of social bonding or solidarity. This component will thus be referred to as the Solidarity Factor.

Factor 2, on the other hand, stresses ability or effectiveness (Osgood's Potency). Intelligence, cultivation, self-confidence, and leadership are all qualities associated with high status, prestige, or power. This component will be referred to here as the Status Factor.

Factor 3 is more restricted, with high loadings only from ambition and pride. This factor was therefore much less powerful in explaining the variance in the original data set. It seems to correspond to Osgood's "Activity," and might be labeled "Egotism," since this is a culturally important concept in Barcelona. This factor was subjected to the same kind of analysis of variance as the other two. However, both because it contributes so little to explaining the original data set, and because it was not taken into account in the initial formulation of guiding hypotheses, the analysis of this third factor will not be detailed in the rest of this report.

Using the factor coefficients for each original trait generated by the Varimax rotation, the original judgment data were reduced to factor scores on each of the three main factors.* The outcome of the completed factor analysis is a set of scores on three factors instead of on fifteen traits. The number of cases, 1,824 (228 respondents × 8 voices), remains the same, but the data are now both more manageable and more comprehensible.

Analysis of Variance. To see what effect the language used (and other variables) had on the factor scores, they were analyzed using techniques of analysis of variance (ANOVA). The analysis asks whether the mean scores on a variable differ significantly from one group (or group of observations) to another, taking into account variation within groups as well as between groups (Iverson and Norpoth 1976: 8).†

In the analysis of variance reported here, the effects of three independent variables were tested. The first was respondents' language affiliation (RL) as defined by reported home language use, with two possible values, Catalan (CT) and Castilian (CS). The second was the language used by the speaker (L), again with only two values, CT and CS. The third independent variable was the speaker (S), with four values, one for each speaker.‡

Three-way analysis of variance (RL × L × S) was conducted separately on each of the two factors, Solidarity and Status. The results for each factor were quite different, as hypothesized, and will be discussed separately.

Solidarity

In the analysis of the Solidarity Factor, the following effects were statistically significant: a main effect for Language alone, a main ef-

---

*In calculating the factor scores, missing observations for a particular original variable were replaced by the mean of the variable. This is a conservative method of dealing with missing data that tends to reduce the magnitude of the factor scores (Kim 1975: 489).

†The analysis of variance was carried out using BMDP program P2V for repeated-measure models (Dixon and Brown 1977).

‡In earlier explorations of the data, it was hypothesized that a fourth variable, R's sex, might affect the scores, since many researchers have found evidence of different language attitudes and behavior in men and women (Labov 1966b, Gal 1978, Lambert 1967, Milroy 1980). In both ANOVA and MANOVA analyses of factor scores arrived at through slightly different calculations, no significant effect for sex was found. The hypothesis was rejected, and that variable is not included in the analysis discussed here.

TABLE 5.4
Analysis of Variance, Solidarity Factor

Variable	Sum of squares	Degrees of freedom	F	Probability
Language (L)	4.48892	1	5.563	.019
Speaker (S)	43.58365	3	13.654	<.001
L × RL[a]	21.45798	1	26.592	<.001
L × S	27.79321	3	16.875	<.001

[a] In this table and Table 5.7, RL = Respondent's Language, as opposed to L = Language used by the speaker.

fect for Speaker alone, an interaction effect for Language with Respondent's Language (L × RL), and an interaction effect for Speaker and Language (S × L; see Table 5.4).

The main effect for Language alone derives from the fact that, overall, respondents gave higher Solidarity ratings to speakers when they used Castilian (mean score, .0798) than when they used Catalan (mean score, −.0798). This effect must be discounted, however, because the interaction effect of L × RL shows that each respondent group favored its own native language. Since the respondent sample was biased toward Castilian speakers, the main effect of preference for Castilian must be considered an artifact of sampling rather than an accurate reflection of a general preference.

The significant main effect for Speaker indicates that some speaker or speakers tended to receive higher overall Solidarity ratings than others, no matter which language they used or which group was doing the rating. To determine where this difference lay, or which speaker(s) differed significantly from the others, a Newman-Keuls post-hoc test of multiple comparisons was used. It was found that Speaker 2, Dolores, was the single speaker responsible for this effect. She had significantly ($p < .01$) higher ratings than all the others, who did not differ significantly from each other.

At least two explanations for this effect can be posited. First, there may be some idiosyncratic features of Dolores's voice or speech style that are appreciated by all respondents and carry across languages. Certainly it is true that Dolores has, in impressionistic terms, a soft but lively voice that several people listening to the tape noted as especially appealing, so this might well be the correct explanation. Second, and alternatively, Dolores is the one speaker who comes closest to being an unmarked, balanced bilingual. As mentioned above, her Castilian is clearly that of a native speaker, and her Catalan can almost pass as native in spite of being marked by Castilian interference. Her higher overall score may reflect the fact that she was able to pick up fairly high ratings in at least one instance from each group for this reason. (See the discussion of the interaction effects, below.) In the absence of data for a much larger number of speakers, we cannot choose between these interpretations and decide whether the Speaker effect is idiosyncratic or socially conditioned. Still, this problem does not interfere with the exploration of our main question, the effect of language choice, since each speaker was presented in each language.

More interesting and relevant to the questions at hand are the interaction effects between Respondent's Language and Language used (RL × L), and between Speaker and Language (S × L). An interaction effect means that a particular independent variable has a different effect on one group of scores than on another, as grouped by the second independent variable. Mean scores must be looked at to discover what the relationship is. Examination of the mean scores reveals that Catalan respondents gave higher ratings to the Catalan language guises while Castilian respondents gave higher ratings to the Castilian guises:

| | Respondent's language | |
Language	Catalan	Castilian
Catalan	.12245	−.20006
Castilian	.00297	.12680

A preference is registered by both groups, but is more marked for the Castilian respondents. This RL × L effect might be said to indicate the following principle: "People who speak the hearer's language evoke greater feelings of solidarity."

But the second interaction effect must also be considered. The S × L effect means that the preference for a particular language depends not just on who is listening, but on who is speaking. We can make sense of this if we posit that respondents are aware of the habitual language of the speaker as signaled through accent cues and intonation patterns, and that these linguistic identities enter into the evaluation process.

To represent this effect, mean scores were calculated according to whether the speakers were dominant Catalan or Castilian speakers, as well as which language they used. In the tabulation below, we see that the mean scores are higher for the Castilian-dominant speakers when they use Castilian, and for the Catalan-dominant speakers when they use Catalan.

Language	Speaker's dominant language	
	Catalan	Castilian
Catalan	−.01822	−.14140
Castilian	−.09478	.25443

A second principle seems to be in effect: "People who speak their own language evoke greater feelings of solidarity."

This first interpretation of the two interaction effects makes it appear that there are two separate principles that enter into conflict when the habitual language of a speaker is not the same as the habitual language of the hearer. However, this interpretation is somewhat misleading; a more coherent picture emerges if we look from a different perspective at how these two effects add up.

The mean scores when the data are partitioned according to the two principles identified above are given below. The horizontal axis shows whether the speaker is using her own language (+) or not (−); on the vertical axis, the scores are divided according to whether the speaker is using the respondent's language (+) or not (−).

Speaker uses respondent's language	Speaker uses own dominant language	
	+	−
+	.2874	−.0369
−	−.0512	−.1992

Looking at these scores, we can see that the principles given above derive primarily from the reactions to the speech behavior of co-members of the linguistic group. The scores are very high when the speaker is using a language that is both her own and the respondent's; i.e., she is a member of the respondent's group using the ingroup language. The scores are very low when the speaker uses a language that is neither her own nor the respondent's; i.e., she is a member of the respondent's group using the outgroup language. Speakers who use a language that is their own but not the respondent's, or the respondent's language but not their own, are speakers who are not co-members of the respondent's group. These two situations evoke ratings that are both undifferentiated from each other and relatively neutral in contrast to the other two mean scores.

These mean scores tell us that respondents assign the highest Solidarity ratings to speakers who are co-members of their own language group and who use the group language. They are basically neutral in their response to speakers who are members of the outgroup, and it does not matter which language these speakers use. Most important, respondents penalize co-members of their group who use the outgroup rather than the ingroup language by giving them the lowest Solidarity scores. Not only do they rate much less solidarity when they use the outgroup language than when they use the ingroup language, but they are even given much lower ratings than the members of the outgroup.

This interpretation of the results rests on the assumption that it is clues to a speaker's underlying identity that create the $S \times L$ effect. This is not an unreasonable claim, since it both accords with the principles of language and identity outlined in Chapters 3 and 4 and accounts most parsimoniously for the data. However, this is a rather large claim to be based on so small a sample of speakers. It is possible that there is something else about each speaker's voice, something idiosyncratic, that coincidentally gives rise to the pattern in the results. In the absence of further data on more speakers, both the parsimony and the plausibility of the identity explanation make it worth retaining.

Another caveat is that the overall results discussed above could be created by the strength of reactions to only one or two speakers rather than all four. For this reason, it was considered worthwhile to break the Solidarity scores out for each Speaker to identify where the major differences lay.

For each Speaker, a "Difference Score" was calculated, representing the difference between the ratings of her Catalan and Castilian guises, as evaluated by each of the Respondent groups. These scores are given in Table 5.5. The sign of the scores indicates the direction of favorability. If the Catalan score is higher than the Castilian, the sign is positive; if the Castilian score is higher than the Catalan, the sign is negative. Paired-sample t-scores were calculated for each of these Difference Scores, and the t-scores and their associated probabilities are reported in Table 5.6.

From these scores, we can see that the pattern of preference for

TABLE 5.5
Difference Scores, Solidarity Factor

Respondents	Speaker			
	1 Angeles (Andal.)	2 Dolores (Cast.)	3 Montse (Cat.)	4 Núria (Cat.)
Castilian	−.7200	−.5091	.0440	−.1225
Catalan	−.1425	.0865	.4889	.0539

TABLE 5.6
T-Scores and Associated
Probabilities of Difference Scores, Solidarity Factor

Respondents	Speaker			
	1	2	3	4
Castilian	−7.358 ($p<.001$)	−6.283 ($p<.001$)	0.444 ($p=.655$)	−1.265 ($p=.208$)
Catalan	−1.256 ($p=.213$)	0.900 ($p=.371$)	3.590 ($p=.001$)	0.451 ($p=.653$)

NOTE: When several tests of significance are performed simultaneously, in order to maintain the chosen alpha level, e.g. .01 or .05 overall, that figure must be divided by the number of tests performed. In this case, where eight tests have been carried out, to maintain an overall level of .05, for any particular test, $p<.0063$; for an overall .01, individual $p<.0014$.

language loyalty within the ingroup and indifference to language choice among the outgroup holds true in all but one instance. Castilian respondents favor the Castilian guise of both the Andalusian speaker, Angeles (S1), and the standard Castilian speaker, Dolores (S2). Language choice has no significant effect on their evaluation of the Catalan-dominant speakers, Montse and Núria (S3 and S4).

Catalan respondents follow the pattern of registering no significant differences in response to language choice on the part of native Castilian speakers. In this aspect, the attitude toward the outgroup is similar to that of the Castilian respondents. But whereas the effect of preference for the ingroup language operates for Speaker 3, the urban Catalan, it does not apply to Speaker 4, the provincial Catalan.

It is possible that the Catalan respondents do not identify with the provincial accent of Speaker 4, and thus that they do not identify her as a member of their ingroup. Some Catalan speakers from areas outside Barcelona have claimed that this is becoming the result of the elevation of Barcelona Catalan to an oral standard. This would mean that Catalans have a much narrower definition of the "We" group than do Castilians, who apply the same principle to both an Andalusian and a standard Castilian, despite the much greater dialect differences between them.

An alternative explanation is that Speaker 4 makes her Catalan identity so very clear in either language that she is not penalized when she speaks Castilian. Both of these explanations are pure conjecture, and again more speakers would have to be tested to draw any conclusions.

Though the Catalan respondents' reaction to Speaker 4 does not support the pattern established in the other cases, neither does it run counter to this pattern. The direction of favorability is toward the Catalan guise in this instance; it is simply not great enough to be significant. Therefore, on the strength of the overall evidence, we can continue to accept the Language–Identity explanation I developed above, with some confidence as it applies to Castilians and some reservations as it applies to Catalans.

Status

The results of the analysis of the Status factor were quite different from those of the Solidarity factor. Significant effects were found only for the following variables: a main effect for Language, a main effect for Speaker, and some evidence of an interaction effect for Speaker × Respondent's Language (Table 5.7). There were no interaction effects of Language with either Respondent's Language or Speaker, an important difference from the results on the Solidarity factor.

Though the F value for the Speaker effect is massive and must not be ignored, the main effect for Language is by far the most important for the questions this study asks. In contrast to the Language effect for Solidarity, in which Castilian was favored and which could be attributed to the weighting of the sample, it is Catalan that receives significantly higher Status ratings (mean Catalan score, .04150, mean Castilian score, −.04146). Since there is no interaction effect with Respondent's Language, there is no reason to believe that this higher evaluation of Catalan is not shared by both Catalans and Castilians.

TABLE 5.7
Analysis of Variance, Status Factor

Variable	Sum of squares	Degrees of freedom	F	Probability
Language	3.48954	1	5.829	.017
Speaker	456.64770	3	210.594	<.001
S×RL	6.00655	3	2.770	.041

This result runs counter to the expectation of language planners and sociolinguists who focus on the importance of the legal order and institutional sanctions in determining the status or prestige of a language. In that model, it was Castilian that could be expected to receive higher Status ratings. Moreover, given the sample bias toward Castilian speakers and the bias against Catalan that may have been introduced by the use of the school domain and a formal text, as discussed above, the dominance of Catalan in the Status ratings is a noteworthy result.

Since there was some evidence of an interaction effect between S and RL, in interpreting the Speaker effect the scores were broken out by Respondent group. It happens that there is agreement between the two groups on the rank ordering of the four speakers, and the interaction effect is the result of the fact that Catalan respondents assigned more extreme scores in both directions than the Castilian respondents did. In order to pinpoint where the differences among the speakers lay, a Newman-Keuls test was again performed on the mean overall scores of each speaker. Because a greater number of significant differences were found in this case than for the Solidarity factor, the scores are presented (Tables 5.8–5.9).

All the speakers differed significantly from each other except Speaker 4, Núria, and Speaker 2, Dolores. Because Núria is the most Catalan of the speakers, and Dolores is the most Castilian, there is no evidence that being a native speaker of either language disqualifies people from being seen as having high status.

Speaker 1, Angeles, received Status scores drastically lower than the others. Again, we cannot know from this small sample of speakers whether these differences are idiosyncratic or socially conditioned. Angeles is the Andalusian speaker, and Andalusian dialects of Castilian are generally stigmatized throughout the northern regions of Spain. It is likely that Angeles's very low ratings are evidence

TABLE 5.8
Ordered Mean Status Scores of Speakers

Speaker	Castilian respondents	Catalan respondents
S1, Angeles (Andalusian)	−.7889	−.9454
S3, Montse (Catalan)	.1460	−.0256
S4, Núria (Catalan)	.3042	.3475
S2, Dolores (Castilian)	.4089	.5056

TABLE 5.9
Absolute Difference Between Speakers' Status Scores

Respondent group	S1	S3	S4	S2
Castilian respondents				
S1	—	0.9349**	1.0931**	1.1978**
S3		—	0.1582*	0.2628**
S4			—	0.1046
S2				—
Catalan respondents				
S1	—	0.9198**	1.2929**	1.4510**
S3		—	0.3731**	0.5312**
S4			—	0.1581
S2				—

* = significant at .05; ** = significant at .01, Newman-Keuls test.

of this stigmatization, even from Castilian speakers who are themselves of Andalusian origin (echoing Lambert's findings for French Canadians in Quebec). It is also true, however, that her pitch, breathing, and intonation patterns differed considerably from the other speakers. Some of these features may be idiosyncratic and may be responsible for her extremely low ratings.

That Angeles would receive such poor Status scores was evident from the time the experiment was run; in every classroom, laughter broke out at the sound of Angeles's first sentence in Castilian. When, in follow-up discussion with the respondents, I asked why this happened, several pointed specifically to the accent and to the "margination" of Andalusian immigrants in Catalonia. Yet one immigrant informant told me she knew she rated the Andalusian as less intelligent, "not because I think Andalusians are less intelligent, but because she *sounded* less intelligent." We cannot know whether this judgment arises from an unconscious association between Andalusian speech patterns and lower status and social honor, or from features peculiar to Angeles, although it seems very likely that it is socially conditioned.

Summary Discussion: Status and Solidarity

In sum, the results for the Status factor demonstrate that some speakers are accorded more status honor or prestige than others, no matter which language they speak, and that this difference does not necessarily depend on underlying language identity. A Castilian and a Catalan can be rated equally highly, showing that individual features of a speaker can be more important than ethnolinguistic considerations in determining personal prestige. Nonetheless, the choice of language can enhance or detract from a speaker's self-presentation and basic claim to status. It is not the institutional value of Castilian that enhances the perceived authority and prestige of a speaker; rather, there is significant evidence that the use of the Catalan language creates this effect. With Weber, we can say that the legal order may attempt to guarantee power and honor, but it is not necessarily their primary source. The legal order is an additional factor that enhances the chance to hold power or honor, but it cannot always secure them (1958: 180–81). In the Catalan case, the Castilianist legal order has not been able to secure linguistic prestige.

The failure of formal policies to establish prestige forces our attention toward the effects of primary economic relations on arrangements for everyday living, and on the structures of experience in daily life. I argue that it is the greater economic power of Catalans that is the basis for the assignment of linguistic prestige; it is *who* speaks a language rather than *where* it is spoken that gives it its force. Authority is established and inculcated most thoroughly not in schools and other formal institutions, but in personal relations, face-to-face encounters, and the invidious distinctions of the workplace and residential neighborhoods.

It might be countered that the strong national consciousness of Catalonia and organized political resistance to Castilian rule are the more critical factors. Certainly it is true that although Castile and Castilian have long held power in the legal order, this power was not in fact recognized as legitimate by much of the Catalan population; power was therefore not necessarily perceived as authority (Woolard

1985a). Nationalist movements and the conscious organization of language loyalty resulting from such movements have been credited with upgrading the value of languages in other parts of the world (e.g. Roberts and Williams 1980 for Wales, though it is not clear whether such increased value is primarily in terms of status or solidarity).

These movements, however, are usually claimed to affect only the attitudes of speakers of the language in question; it is more difficult to see how they would be effective in changing the attitudes of the outgroup. In the Status ratings described above, no difference was found between Catalan and Castilian attitudes toward the two languages; Catalan was recognized by both groups as the more prestigious and higher-status language. Additionally, my interpretation is at least partially supported by the comments of many immigrant informants themselves, who revealed that they based their evaluation of the Catalan language on its speakers rather than on its uses. Ignacio said he thought that Catalan would emerge as more prestigious because "a person who knows Catalan could know other things, too." Consuelo, one of the adult education students and a factory worker, volunteered that "Catalans not only *sound* more cultivated and refined; they *are*."

I would therefore argue that the greater prestige of Catalan does not depend on the political nationalism found in Catalonia, but rather co-varies with it, and that both depend on the economic strength of the region and its natives (cf. Vilar 1979a). We cannot decide between the explanatory value of these two positions at this point in history by examining the Catalan case alone. Nonetheless, the most important point still stands: the legal order does not always secure honor and prestige, whether for reasons of economics or legitimacy. Therefore, in approaching the study of minority languages, we cannot make assumptions about people's attitudes toward a language's prestige value on the basis of institutional hegemony. And if we wish to effect changes in people's attitudes toward a language in order to affect their behavior (as in minority movements for mother-tongue education, or the English-only movement in the United States), we cannot necessarily expect changes in institutional policy to be sufficient. The work of making meanings in social life responds to far more than just the messages of the formal media and institutions of communication in society.

Solidarity operates according to a different logic. In the experiment, respondents appear to negatively sanction linguistic cooptation on the part of members of their own linguistic group, though they are largely indifferent to the language behavior of the other group. Ingroup members are rewarded for loyalty to the group language by increased solidarity ratings when they speak it, and penalized for betrayal. But outgroup members are not rewarded with increased solidarity for venturing to use the other language when it can be detected that they are outsiders, as the preference for hearing one's own language might have led us to believe.*

The significantly different results for Dolores compared with other speakers shows that the characteristics valued for solidarity are not attributed solely along linguistic group lines, at least not by the Catalans. Idiosyncrasies of "personality" are detected in voices and affect people's responses. Ingroup members, however, can enhance or reduce the feelings of solidarity they elicit by manipulation of language choice, whereas the outgroup cannot. Thus it seems that there is no immediate payoff in increased social acceptance from the outgroup in return for using their language, though there is considerable risk of loss of support from the linguistic group of origin. This could well be a critical factor in determining patterns of language acquisition and use.

The results of the language attitudes test must be interpreted and generalized with some caution, as must all experimental results. They were produced in an unnatural situation, and respondents were forced to make judgments that they conceivably might suspend in the initial stages of interaction. Few respondents hesitated to make such judgments, however, and there is much outside evidence that shows that initial impressions not only are critical in establishing the outcome of an interaction, but are often formed in large part on the basis of linguistic self-presentation (Gumperz 1982, Murray 1981, Cook-Gumperz 1981). Another consideration is that the test was limited

---

*It is quite possible that while anticipatory linguistic accommodation to Catalans is not greeted with greater solidarity, overt situational accommodation could be received quite differently. The test tells us nothing about how speakers are perceived if within an interaction they shift from Castilian to Catalan to accommodate the interlocutor (or vice versa). In such circumstances, solidarity might indeed be enhanced, as predicted by accommodation theory (Giles and Powesland 1975). This would mean, however, that a speaker would receive the greatest benefits, not by assimilating to the Catalan language, but by preserving a basic Castilian linguistic identity from which advantageous shifts could be made.

to the representation of a single speech event, a formal monologue in a school setting. Though this might be an appropriate way to measure status or prestige, it might not be equally apt for measuring solidarity. Students, after all, are ideally expected to respect their teachers, but not necessarily to like or identify with them. Nonetheless, language use did seem to affect feelings of solidarity even in this formal circumstance, and it is reasonable to assume that such effects would only be heightened, not lessened, in other circumstances.

With these caveats in mind, and taken together with ethnographic evidence, the values of the two languages revealed by the matched-guise test can help explain patterns of language maintenance and second-language acquisition in Barcelona. We can posit that language attitudes are indirectly fed back to speakers in interaction by influencing the way in which listeners respond, and therefore influencing the outcome of exchanges. Speakers' behavior is also affected by their own attitudes, since speakers are also their own auditors (Smith, Giles, and Hewstone 1978). As Consuelo put it, "I sound more intelligent to myself when I speak Catalan." The following chapter will examine the effect of these language attitudes on language behavior in Barcelona, and consider their implications for ethnolinguistic problems encountered in other settings.

CHAPTER SIX |||| EXPLAINING
LINGUISTIC CHOICES
AND ETHNIC PROCESS

The durability of Catalan has been an impetus for the question, "Why do low-prestige languages persist?," and for the claim that solidarity can override status in determining linguistic choices. From a perspective that gives central importance to the legal order and institutional dominance, the remarkable fact in need of explanation has been the maintenance of Catalan, and its extension to some immigrants, despite the institutional power and prestige of Castilian.

The results of the matched-guise experiment turn this commonsense view of the situation in Catalonia on its head. We can see that the question, "Why do low-prestige languages persist?," is not appropriately asked about Catalan, which is not a low-prestige language in people's minds or ears, as has been supposed. The higher status of Catalan helps explain why Catalonia is almost unique among European minority languages in maintaining and even recruiting speakers.* It is not necessary to posit that Catalans were

---

*A European minority situation similar to that of Catalonia might be Alsace. Alsace is also an economically and industrially advanced zone in a larger state, and native speakers have maintained Alsatian to a similar, if not equal, degree (Verdoodt 1972, Gaines 1978). The link between the economic order and language maintenance seems to be supported. However, language is not as politicized an issue in Alsace as in Catalonia, and there is some evidence that young Alsatians are more likely to introduce

somehow more solidary or more responsive to group pressures than the Welsh, the Irish, the Hungarians of Austria, the Gaelic speakers of Scotland, or even Catalan speakers in Valencia and in the Rousillon of France who did shift away from Catalan. Rather, we see that in addition to symbolizing group solidarity, the Catalan language in Catalonia has the advantage of symbolizing high status. These experimental findings also make clear why we do not find more metaphorical conversational codeswitching among Catalans. There are no additional prestigious connotations to motivate a switch to Castilian for rhetorical effect, and there are indeed solidarity sanctions against it.

In addition to making sense of the formerly puzzling maintenance of the Catalan language by Catalans, the investigation of language attitudes also can help us to make sense of the behavior of Castilian-speaking immigrants. Surveys have shown that the overwhelming majority of immigrant parents want their children to learn Catalan (Badia i Margarit 1969, Torres 1980: 52–53). This is to be expected in view of the prestige value of the language. Yet the proportion of their children who actually learn Catalan does not seem to be nearly as high, and those who adopt Catalan for informal and intimate use are very much in the minority. Given the high status of Catalan, the question is not why recent generations of Catalans have not shifted to Castilian, but rather why more young Castilian immigrants and second-generation immigrants do not actively use Catalan.

Other researchers have shown that the desire or need to identify oneself with a particular group or network may motivate speakers to resist the pressures of linguistic prestige (Labov 1966b, Trudgill 1972, Gal 1979, Dorian 1981, Milroy 1980). The subtle process of differentiation revealed by the Solidarity measure in the Barcelona matched-guise test provides a new key that helps us make this motivation even clearer.

By reacting to language choice with greater or lesser solidarity, listeners patrol the linguistic border, discouraging co-members from changing their linguistic patterns. This point, revealed in the atti-

French into the home during adolescence (Cole 1975). As reported by Verdoodt and by Gaines, Alsace differs from Catalonia in several important respects: its religious divisions, which crosscut linguistic boundaries; its historical association with two different states; its vernacular language, which is associated with another dialect of German as a written standard; and its much lower rate of immigration from the larger state. According to Verdoodt, French immigrants constitute only 4 percent of the Alsatian population.

tudes test, confirms the earlier research. But additionally, in Catalonia we find that the two linguistic groups, in their role of informal communities rather than political constituencies, do not actively recruit new members from across the linguistic boundaries. There is no increased social acceptance from the target group to compensate for the penalty imposed by the original group when a speaker whose linguistic origins are still identifiable attempts the other language. Immediate benefits do not outweigh immediate risks in change of language orientation.

Ethnographic evidence and informants' reports illustrate the way these forces for ethnolinguistic maintenance and against recruitment work in interaction. The traditional "polite" Catalan switch to Castilian in talking to a person who has revealed a Castilian identity, described in Chapter 4, is the interactional enactment of this complex solidarity phenomenon. A more negative sanction that can actively reinforce linguistic boundaries is ridicule. Castilians often claim that they are afraid to speak Catalan because Catalans ridicule their mistakes. Yet when I asked each informant if he or she had ever been laughed at by Catalans, few could answer that they had, and none could give a specific example. The notion of Catalan ridicule may be largely a myth passed among the Castilian language group. Instead, several students claimed that in their twice-weekly Catalan class, it is the Castilian speakers, not the Catalans, who laugh at the accents and mistakes of those who attempt to speak the language. This is consistent with the ingroup solidarity sanctions found in the matched-guise test.

If there are strong solidarity forces against the linguistic assimilation of Castilians, the question arises why some Castilian speakers learn Catalan while many do not. Who are these people? Are they those who are able to defer gratification and are motivated by the promise of long-term status rewards in spite of short-term losses? Or are there social differences rather than simply individual differences between learners and nonlearners? This is the question that will be explored in the following sections of this chapter.

Who Learns Catalan?

Among my informants whose linguistic repertoire I could confirm by observation as well as whose life history I obtained in interview, fifteen were Castilians (age range approximately fifteen–thirty-five) who had learned Catalan and used it consistently in at least some part of their daily lives. Six more were in the process of consciously learning to speak Catalan, either by taking voluntary classes, practicing with a specific group of Catalans, or seeking out situations in which to practice. Although the sample is not representative or systematic, and generalizations based on the experiences of only twenty-one people are of necessity tentative, certain patterns are evident, suggestive, and worthy of discussion.

Of these twenty-one informants, only three had learned Catalan as very small children. The first of these is quite unusual, being the son of upper-middle-class Castilians who for reasons of political and social sympathy sent their children to a clandestine Catalan school in the 1950's and 1960's. The other two were raised in Catalan neighborhoods and learned the language without conscious effort. Castilian-speaking children who are born into predominantly Catalan neighborhoods may easily and seemingly "naturally" acquire native-like competence from their playmates. But because of the tendency toward residential segregation, I encountered relatively few Castilians who had acquired Catalan from neighbors as small children. Most of my Castilian informants—as is true of the majority of Castilians in the Barcelona area—grew up in immigrant enclaves and thus did not have such an opportunity.

Even those who had some Catalan neighbors in a mixed neighborhood rarely learned Catalan. The traditional linguistic etiquette sometimes makes almost a secret world of Catalan, which may vanish from the hearing of Castilian speakers who are not part of the intimate circle. Helena, the young mother of Chapter 3, reported that it was only when she learned Catalan as a teenager that she even realized there were Catalan-speaking families in her apartment building. She had never been aware of the Catalan language in her environment, except from a very elderly neighbor whose age made the language seem like "pure folklore."

The remaining eighteen Castilians who learned or were learning Catalan after early childhood can be divided into two categories. The first category consists of those whose acquisition of Catalan came after their entrance into a well-defined peer group composed almost entirely of Catalans. The second category consists of those who either made a deliberate effort to find settings in which to speak Catalan, or who learned it in ethnically mixed settings rather than closed Catalan groups. The important point in the distinction between the two types of learners is that of the eleven people in the latter category, whom I call "anticipatory learners," only one was a native of Catalonia. The earliest that any of them had immigrated was at the age of eight.

The Barcelona-born among my informants and those who had been brought to Catalonia as infants did not speak Catalan unless they were raised in Catalan neighborhoods or at a later point in life became part of a Catalan group through a change in social circumstances. Other researchers have also found that becoming a member of a social network defined as Catalan was practically the only means by which a Castilian acquired active competence in Catalan in contemporary Barcelona (Strubell i Trueta 1981b; cf. Bastardas 1985, 1986). In 1980, nativeborn teenagers who had studied Catalan in the classroom for up to four years rarely spoke a word outside of class, and some did not even use Catalan during language class.

This difference between immigrants and Barcelona-born Castilian speakers in my small sample is illustrated by the two high school classmates, Josefina and Ignacio, who were profiled in Chapter 3.

Josefina is the teenager who had immigrated to Barcelona with her family when she was eight years old, and who, at fifteen, decided to "catalanize" herself after finding that she was teasingly called "the Catalan girl" when she visited her home village in Albacete. Although she lives in a working-class, overwhelmingly Castilian-speaking dormitory city, she felt Catalan and was anxious to learn Catalan. Josefina took a job in a butcher shop, where she insisted that the Catalan owners and customers should speak Catalan to her. She also asked her few Catalan classmates to speak to her in Catalan, but they admitted in discussion that they found it nearly impossible to do so, because of the force the traditional etiquette carried for them. Josefina claims to have no trouble with Catalan comprehension, and points out that in any case it is easy enough to ask about the meaning of a particular word she might not know. She never mentioned fear of ridicule; all learners make mistakes, she says, and Josefina takes any laughter these might elicit as sympathetic.

Josefina gives two reasons for learning Catalan: one, to be fully integrated into Catalonia; and two, for social and economic advantage. She believes that job possibilities, particularly in the service sector, are greater for those who speak Catalan. Thus, for both symbolic and practical purposes, she wants very much to "become Catalan."

In contrast is Josefina's classmate Ignacio, who claims to know that he is Catalan by birthplace, but does not feel Catalan. In spite of living all his sixteen years in Barcelona, Ignacio does not speak Catalan. Unlike Josefina, he is insecure about his comprehension of Catalan. Ignacio qualified his answers to my questions about what he does when he is addressed in Catalan, saying "*If* I understand the person. . . ." He worries that he might not understand his teachers if they were to use Catalan in class.

Like Josefina, Ignacio evaluates Catalan highly and attributes prestige to its speakers. As he poignantly put it, "Someone who knows Catalan could know other things too." But Ignacio rejects Josefina's belief that learning Catalan could open up more job opportunities. He analyzes social divisions differently than Josefina, seeing ethnicity and social background rather than the language per se as the keys to higher social status. And so, unlike Josefina, Ignacio never attempted to speak Catalan himself.

It appears that the native-born are less likely to learn Catalan in order to break into Catalan networks or establish relations with Catalans, i.e. as a tool for social promotion. Instead, they tend to learn it, if at all, only after they find themselves in such relations and it becomes necessary to speak Catalan to preserve their place. Their behavior confirms Labov's claim that "variation in linguistic behavior does not . . . affect drastically the life chances of the individual; on the contrary, the shape of linguistic behavior changes rapidly as the speaker's social position changes" (1972: 111). Some of the changes in social position that can induce Castilians to speak Catalan are discussed below.

Voluntary organizations. Some Castilians enter into their first contact with Catalan circles in adolescence, when they change schools or join recreation groups. If these changes constitute a sufficiently strong commitment to a new network of peers, they can bring about language change. Helena, who had been unconscious of Catalan in her environment, joined a Girl Scout troop at the age of thirteen. The troop was not only entirely Catalan but explicitly Catalanist in outlook. She remembers passing a year in adolescent agony, often unable to understand or speak to her companions, who would never direct a word to her in Castilian. She remained with the group because it seemed her only opportunity to get out of the house and escape from an isolated childhood. Feeling forced to learn Catalan to participate, she recalls the other Scouts laughing at her mistakes when she began to speak it. But within two years she had gained adequate fluency to become firmly accepted as a full member of the group and to be selected as a leader.

The workplace. Other Castilian informants felt overt or tacit pressure to learn and use Catalan because their places of employment were predominantly Catalan. Such pressure can be exerted more or less gracefully and can engender more or less resentment on the part of the learner. In large part it relies on the accommodation norm; Castilians feel "pressured" to speak Catalan when Catalans no longer accommodate to them by speaking Castilian. At times, however, the requirement can be made explicit. Consuelo (Chap. 3) began to work at the age of thirteen in a textile factory, where she remembers about 80 percent of the workers being Catalan. She reports that her coworkers would tell her, "You, Murciana, if you don't speak Catalan, we're not going to talk to you." She felt this was offered in good humor, and although it was sometimes an effort, she took it in kind, learning to speak Catalan.

Several Castilian informants, professionals in their thirties, worked in institutions with a Catalan nationalist bent and had become speakers of Catalan in recent years. Some wished to do so to symbolize their sympathy with Catalanism, but others commented spontaneously that they wanted to speak the group language to solidify their relations with their colleagues. These converts feel that the transition, though not easy, was made less difficult by the good-natured but firm support and encouragement they received from colleagues and friends.

In contrast, Antonio, a young engineer who was recently promoted in the Barcelona office of a multinational corporation, found that his coworkers and clients were now predominantly Catalan. Although his own mother is Catalan, he had never been a Catalan speaker. He felt that he was being pressured against his will to use Catalan in order to be successful in his work; in his case a strong reaction set in. Antonio decided that he not only preferred the Castilian language, but also preferred the "Castilian character" over the "Catalan character." For Antonio, although part Catalan himself, the felt pressure to become a Catalan speaker had brought to the fore the ethnic stereotypes discussed in Chapter 3.

From the limited number of cases I encountered, it appears that Castilians who find themselves in a predominantly Catalan social environment can and do learn Catalan. They break into these social circles not by deliberate planning but by accident—through a troop or job assignment, in the examples we have seen. Once in the circle, however, they are confronted with the need to learn Catalan if they wish to hold their place.

The structure of the "pressuring" group may have an effect on the newcomer's response. My Barcelona-born informants who learned Catalan after childhood did so in explicitly egalitarian, nonhierarchical settings, where linguistic pressure came from peers, not superordinates. Fellow Girl Scouts and coworkers who shared rank and responsibility were able to affect their new colleagues' language habits. In hierarchical settings where the need for change seems to come from the structure of dominance, pressure may be less successful. It is not only in the hierarchical workplace that Castilian speakers resisted and resented the pressure toward Catalan. Castilian high school students sometimes resented what they saw as the condescending and imperious attitude of the "cultural propaganda" that teachers gave them in their Catalan language classes, the exhortations to learn about "our culture" and "our country."

The importance of the structure of the social setting in creating patterns of resistance or acceptance is in turn reflective of the association of language differences with class differences. In a society where linguistic and class divisions largely coincide, pressures for linguistic assimilation may be interpreted in terms of larger class conflicts. These class associations of the language remain apparent in Catalonia because they are not authorized and legitimized by the legal order, since Catalan does not enjoy institutional dominance. In such a situation, horizontal, peer-originated pressure may be a relatively successful force in promoting language acquisition and integration into the group, whereas pressure from above may provoke backlash. Opportunities or exigencies for language acquisition that are created by those in a position of power may engender more rejection than positive results when they are associated with social and economic inequalities perceived as categorical.

Integrative vs. Instrumental Motivations

This differentiation between hierarchical and egalitarian settings for language learning in class-stratified society is reminiscent of the distinction between instrumental and integrative motivations made by social psychologists. Gardner and Lambert (1972) have posited that integrative motivation (the desire to be accepted by another group) is more effective than instrumental motivation (the desire to get ahead in some way) in the process of second-language acquisition. However, this differentiation of motivations is problematic in the Catalan situation; it is difficult to maintain the distinction between integrative and instrumental motivation.

In societies where the use of a majority language in intergroup interaction does not signal group membership, speakers may actually prefer to use that ethnically "neutral" language in such situations, reserving the minority language for the signaling of solidarity with co-members (Gumperz and Wilson 1971). But in this case, Catalan, the second language in question, is not socially neutral. Catalan is not a public or standard language whose use is a practical necessity in the performance of certain jobs. The pressure for the acquisition of Catalan derives from its status as a restricted, ingroup symbol of an economically and socially dominant group.

The adoption of Catalan for Castilian speakers is not the adoption of a "public voice" to complement the intimate voice of their native language (Rodriguez 1981). Rather, it is the adoption of another, a different, very "private" voice, in the sense that it is still intimately connected with Catalan ethnic identity. Under the social circumstances in 1980, the acquisition of Catalan even on the job was still taken as a sign of "integrative motivation," an implicit signal of a desire to be accepted eventually as a member of the Catalan group.

But because of the ethnic/class structure of the society, the motivation to learn Catalan in hierarchical settings can also be described as essentially instrumental—the desire to succeed in a job, for example. In this case, it is integration—being accepted by a Catalan network—rather than simple language proficiency that is instrumental in obtaining some other valued goal of social promotion. This is closer to the notion of social promotion proposed by Weinreich (1974) when he says that it may be necessary to hide the fact that a language was secondarily acquired. He seems to refer to acceptance as a member of a particular group, and not just mere competence to perform certain tasks. In the Catalan case, at least, it seems unproductive to distinguish the internal motivations of the individual in second-language acquisition. Rather, it is more illuminating to distinguish the external sources of pressure to learn a language and consider their relation to the distribution of dominance in the larger society.

Language Learning: Immigrants vs. Natives

Immigrants may also learn Catalan if they have occasion to enter into a Catalan peer group. And of course many immigrants never learn Catalan at all. But those in my sample were more likely than the native-born to attempt to learn Catalan even under adverse circumstances where conscientious effort was necessary to recruit speaking partners. That is, immigrants were more likely to try to learn Catalan in anticipation of establishing relations with Catalans. First-generation immigrants were also more likely to express positive stereotypes of Catalans and high esteem for Catalonia. Ana (Chap. 3), who thought that all Catalans were intellectually sharper than Castilians, and Josefina, who declared her love and loyalty to Catalonia, are typical examples of this phenomenon; both are "anticipatory" learners of Catalan.

What is the difference between first- and second-generation immigrants that could cause such patterns? We cannot attribute it to some hypothetical "immigrant personality" that might be seen as self-selected for ambition, goal orientation, and resourcefulness. In the case of first-generation immigrants, we are here often speaking of children, who no more controlled their parents' decision to migrate than did the second generation. Nor do the two groups have different family profiles, since they often come from the same regions and differ by only six to ten years in the time of immigration. In fact, the two types sometimes come from the same family.

Josefina has a younger sister who was born in Barcelona and is being taught Catalan in her nursery school. Josefina attempts to speak Catalan to her sister, since she is in need of conversation partners. But the little girl refuses to respond, and according to Josefina, even gets angry when she hears Catalan in her home. The difference between immigrant and native-born appears within this single family.

I suggest that the critical factor determining differences in language behavior is that first-generation immigrants are forced to redefine their social identity and network of social relations when they come to Catalonia. An individual who has severed basic ties in leaving the homeland has less at risk in exploring different possibilities of group membership and the different identities symbolized by language use in Catalonia. Barcelona-born Castilian speakers do not have the same options for the change of identity that the acquisition of the Catalan language seems to imply. Because they live in the social setting in which they were born and among the relationships that they formed from their earliest years, they have more at risk in attempting to change their linguistic identity.

The critical difference I am suggesting does not necessarily lie in differences in the structure of personal networks or even in the ethnicity of the people in them (Milroy 1980, Gal 1979, Gumperz 1958, 1982). Rather, it would lie in the quality of the relationships and the depth of the individual's commitment to them. This quality depends in part on the multiplexity and the time depth of each relation in the network. The important factor is the individual's sense of liberty to create new relationships outside the existing network, his or her evaluation of the potential benefits against the risks to solidarity and support.

First-generation immigrants do not have to betray their identity or their social network in making efforts to assimilate to the Catalan language; they have left the basis of that identity and that network behind. Although they are not necessarily true "lames" in Labov's (1973) sense, they are not full members of any social group when they come to Catalonia. Thus they can take the radical step of refusing to speak Castilian outside their homes or even of leaving Castilian boys on the dance floor, as did Maria, who so successfully transformed herself that her boss accepted her as Catalan. If the linguistically Catalan inhabitants of Catalonia appear to immigrants to be both the most prototypical model of who one can be in the new environment (because they are most different from the region of origin) and the "best" model (because of socioeconomic status), it is of less importance to them that their Castilian-speaking peers may feel less solidary toward them when they begin to use Catalan. As outsiders they did not have full acceptance into or full commitment to the Castilian group in Barcelona anyway, as Josefina's nickname of "La Albacetina" (the girl from Albacete) indicates.

The sense of being a "Castilian" in contrast to and even in conflict with Catalans is one that is formed over time through interaction in

Barcelona, although certain expectations are no doubt brought from the homeland. Within Barcelona, "Castilian" is an emergent, constructed group identity, not a primordial one. Being Castilian in Barcelona still demands change and adjustment of behavior for the immigrant; it is not the same as being Albacetine or Andalusian in the home village (Esteva Fabregat 1973, 1974, 1978). Immigrants are likely to read the social dichotomy of Barcelona differently than the native-born, and to believe that they may as easily change their basic identity from Albacetine or Andalusian to Catalan as from Albacetine or Andalusian to "Castilian" in the sense in which that identity functions in Catalonia.

For second-generation immigrants, the risks carry a very different weight. For people like Ignacio, the effort to become a "real" Catalan implied in learning the language would mean two things: (1) a de facto denial of the legitimacy of his claim to Catalan identity already made on the basis of birthplace and (2) an attempt to "pass," to change one's identity without a legitimizing change in social circumstances. As Dorian notes (1981: 102), adoption of a high-status language is a behavior that clearly signals an attempt to dissociate from a stigmatized group, and as such it is bitterly resented by that group. It is only for those second-generation immigrants who have actually experienced a change in social circumstances that the language-acquisition process is worthwhile. This is true of the eight native-born like Helena who learned Catalan after entering a wholly Catalan group of peers.

The argument I have developed is tentative, built on the observation of some nearly two dozen cases, in combination with the larger-scale experimental work on language attitudes. In summary, on the basis of substantial evidence of different attitudinal responses to language use, I argue that these responses serve as norm-enforcement mechanisms. Different susceptibility to these status motivations and solidarity sanctions may be determined by differing restrictions of social network and social identity. In turn, these differences in identity and commitment to peer group and network are conditioned by whether an individual has immigrated to or has been born into a residentially and socially segregated environment. Immigrants are different not simply because they have different attitudes about the homeland or different values and goals, but because they have to do the interpersonal political work of building new relations and new identity. They have little choice but to take up the task, but they do have choice in how to go about it, and in what identity they aspire to. The native-born do not have these options. Though they may choose to cross over to networks and a linguistic group they were not reared in, they have much more at stake in such a move. They risk the support of the relationships they have developed since birth. Language values affect language behavior, but their impact is mediated by the individual actor's sense of the relative authority of these values in his or her life.

Wider Implications: Some Speculations

The claim that immigrants are both freer and more likely than the native-born to pursue high-status models, whether linguistic or otherwise, is supported by the findings of research in other areas. In a noteworthy parallel, Gans reports that among the Italian-Americans he worked with, the most upwardly mobile individuals were those who had come to America just before their teens. He attributed this mobility to the delayed entry into and marginal attachment of these individuals to their peer groups (1972: 54).

The immigrant/native distinction in the acquisition of Catalan may be relevant to differences between immigrant and native-born minorities in the acquisition of other prestigious forms of behavior. Important differences not only in language acquisition but in school performance between native-born minority children and immigrants have been noted in more than one country. In the United States, differences in school achievement exist not only between immigrant minorities and native subordinate minorities such as Blacks and American Indians, but between immigrant members and U.S.-born members of a particular minority group such as Mexican-Americans, with the age of ten noted by one commentator as a turning point (Carter 1970, cited in Ogbu 1978: 224; Troike 1978).

In a parallel phenomenon, Finnish children who are born in Sweden have been found to trail those who immigrated after the age of ten on several measures of language proficiency and academic skills (Skuttnabb-Kangas 1979, Skuttnabb-Kangas and Toukomaa 1976). The researchers attributed the difference to "semilingualism," the failure to master either language, allegedly created by exposure to a second language before the first was thoroughly inculcated. Interpreted as evidence of the destabilizing effect of early exposure to a second language, particularly as a language of instruction, on cognitive development, this explanation has been applied to the reports of similar phenomena among Mexican-Americans (Troike 1978). The Finnish-Swedish study has been extremely influential internationally in debates about mother-tongue education (Cummins 1979, Edelsky et al. 1983).

There are notable similarities in (1) age of immigration, ten years or over, determining the school success of Finns in Sweden, (2) the preadolescent critical period for immigration noted by Gans, and (3) the immigration age, eight–thirteen, that I found to condition the acquisition of Catalan. In Barcelona it is true that overall school success was not the phenomenon examined, but more simply the acquisition and use of a second language. Nonetheless, the comparison is useful, particularly since in Barcelona the differential language acquisition noted is quite clearly a social and not a cognitive phenomenon. The cognitive effects of language of instruction, at any age, cannot explain differential acquisition of language skills here, since all of the Castilian speakers attended Castilian medium schools. Yet I still found immigration age to have critical effects on behavior, just as in the Finnish study, and I have argued that these should be understood as effects of social relations and social identity. The coincidence in the crucial age of immigration leads me to believe that similar social factors, rather than cognitive-linguistic ones, may also create the noted effects on language proficiency and school success in Sweden and the United States. The Finnish research's emphasis on cognitive factors may be misdirected, as may be social explanations that focus on separate value systems or sources of self-esteem deriving from experiences in the homeland.

Rather than the home environment or the cognitive-linguistic landscape, it may be the host social environment that is differently constructed for those who have to create new ties in a community and those who must defend older ones. Immigrants and natives not only may assign different values to symbolic behavior such as language use or school achievement, they also have different social risks to consider in evaluating the costs and benefits of pursuing prestige models of behavior. These different costs and benefits may lie at the root of the paradoxical process by which differences between groups in contact can become progressively more, not less, entrenched through prolonged exposure. The insights deriving from this study of the social organization of language differences in Barcelona may be useful in understanding ethnolinguistic processes more generally.

Ethnic Process in Catalonia: By Way of Conclusion

An image that captures the situation of Catalonia described in this book is that of the seam created by a sewing machine, joining two pieces of cloth and demarcating the boundary between them at the same time.* From a cursory inspection, a seam appears as a single, well-defined line. But when we look closer, or if we are able to watch the machine as it constructs the seam, we know that this single boundary is in fact made up of two separate threads that cross each other and interlock, one fed through the mechanisms of the bobbin and one fed from the needle. If we use a white thread for the bobbin and a black one for the needle, this becomes more apparent. In a properly sewn seam, against the backdrop of the first piece of cloth, only the white thread will show. If we turn it over, only the black thread of the seam will be seen. But when the tension is improperly set on the sewing machine, the black thread will sometimes show through on the side where only the white should be seen, or vice versa. And any seamstress knows that this is the sign of a weak seam, one that might unravel in little time.

In this elaborate metaphor, the Spanish state and Catalonia are two pieces of cloth both delineated and bound together by the seam of ethnicity. At first glance, the seam appears as a single line differentiating Catalans and Castilians. But against the backdrop of the Spanish state, where it asserts the unity of the region in the face of external power, Catalan ethnicity shows up like a white thread. When we flip the garment over and look at the thread of ethnicity against the background of Catalan society, we find that ethnic phenomena are of an entirely different color.

To belabor the metaphor further, each thread is itself a continuous woven filament of responses to the psychological, social, economic, and political experiences of daily life. Though the two threads of ethnicity are not identical, they do cross and interlock at the point where there is agreement on the use and meaning of certain symbols.

*Bambi Schieffelin first suggested this metaphor for the situation I was trying to describe; she is not to be held responsible for the lengths to which I have taken it.

The thread that stands out against the Spanish state was fed into place largely by the mechanisms of the Spanish centralist state under Franco. For the most part, the experiences of Catalan cultural nationalists and the Castilian-speaking working class are twined together, strengthening this fiber. Against the backdrop of the larger Spanish state, it makes sense for immigrants to say that they "feel Catalan," for two reasons. First, in contrast to the poverty of the regions from which they came, many may indeed embrace the urban standard of living and progressive values associated with Catalonia and with Barcelona in particular. But second, and more important, both the culturally Catalan of Barcelona and the Castilian-speaking working class experienced the reactionary central state of the Franco years as oppressive to their interests, and this understanding of centralism still informs political processes.

As Giner points out (1984: 57), a hegemonic political culture was established in Catalonia, a culture capable of legitimizing certain nationalist courses of action and delegitimizing the superimposed Francoist ideology. But it is not necessarily the case that Castilian-speaking workers set aside their class interests or accept the mystification of Catalan symbols when they support Catalan demands for autonomy. Few are convinced when the conservative president of Catalonia tells them that "all who live and work here are Catalan"; this is not necessarily their motivating force. Against the historical backdrop of centralist policy, it was the very class position of the Castilian immigrants that led them to identify their interests with those of Catalan nationalists as lying in the devolution of the state. Spain as a monolithic entity had not demonstrated sufficient interest in altering the inequities of a highly stratified society; an autonomous region where the leftist and liberal parties have traditionally been strong appeared to many at this juncture as a more amenable arena in which to negotiate infrastructural changes and a redistribution of power and resources.

It is the meaning of Catalanism as liberty and progressivism that allows the use of distinctively Catalan symbols to articulate the struggle against the central state. Such symbols as the Catalan flag, Catalan hymns, and Catalan language slogans were used by both Catalans and Castilians in Barcelona when they turned out as many as a million strong to manifest their will for self-government. Both cultural Catalanists and class-guided Castilian speakers could join in Catalan shouts of "**Visca Catalunya**" (Long live Catalonia) when they were directed against Madrid. But these symbols are those that show up against the backdrop of the Spanish cloth. Participants and analysts who believe that such demonstrations of unity of purpose say anything definitive about the ethnic and linguistic form that an autonomous Catalan society will take may be mistaken.

When we turn the cloth over, Catalan society itself is the backdrop for the interpretation of ethnic experience in all its manifestations, from the personal to the institutional. And in many respects, the passage of the Statute of Autonomy represented a turning of the cloth. Positions regarding ethnicity, and language in particular, taken in the electoral campaigns for the Catalan parliament differed from those of the campaign for the Statute of Autonomy. Immigrant-oriented parties emerged, and Catalanist parties publicly reconsidered their positions on "who is Catalan." Within the now-real frame of a Catalan administrative apparatus, however weak, the question of the relation of different groups within Catalonia came into focus. In this setting, the principal distinction highlighted by symbols of ethnicity was that between those who had come to sell their labor and those who employed them.

Language use and language policy in particular are foregrounded in this context. In symbolizing sentiments of unity to the Spanish state, the actual language of day-to-day activity is not critical. A shout of "**Visca Catalunya**" (when coupled with the proper voting patterns) is sufficient demonstration of unity. Madrid does not actually talk to individual workers. But against the backdrop of Catalan society, such broad-stroke symbols are not meaningful. The language in which people actually talk to each other is a relevant sign of identity and a symbol of competing orientations and interests within Catalan society. It therefore becomes a major point of contention in the elaboration of new social policies by the Catalan government.

The behaviors that are considered appropriate, the positions that can be taken, and the issues that can be debated in Catalonia are constrained by tension between the two processes of self-definition. Each time the Spanish state or the Catalan government increases the tension—the former by threatening to limit the powers of the autonomous governments, the latter by formulating linguistic policies that appear to favor Catalan, for example—the loops of thread begin to show through on the wrong side. So, when Castilian-speaking leaders in Catalonia protest Catalanist linguistic policies, as they did in the linguistic *"Manifiesto"* of the spring of 1981 (Miguel et al. 1981), what should be an internal question shows up awkwardly against the background of the Spanish state. Ideally, such internal dissension should not show through, and when it does, it is taken as a threat—perhaps deliberate, perhaps inadvertent—to the very boundary between Spain and Catalonia (cf. Pedrolo et al. 1981).

For native Catalans, there is continuity between the two sides of the ethnicity issue; the same cultural and linguistic behavior they use to articulate the struggle with the Spanish state articulates for them the vision of the new Catalonia. But Castilian speakers experience a shift in the meaning of the symbols across the two contexts. Whereas in the context of the Spanish state, the Catalan language is an oppressed victim whose rights must be championed, within the context of Catalonia—especially a Catalonia empowered to administer its own affairs—the Catalan language is a reminder of class differences and looks alarmingly like a potential weapon of oppression. Again, the life experiences of Castilian speakers in Barcelona, informed largely by class, determine their outlook, but within Catalan society they have very different implications.

These complexities of ethnic politics in Catalonia point out an important constraint on generalizations about the causes of ethnic conflict. In particular, attempts to understand the relation of class and ethnicity must consider the context of power in which conflicts take place, and in which participants view them as taking place. Different interpretive contexts, such as those provided by nested political frameworks for competition, not only make different aspects of experience relevant, they also can change the meaning of such a constant and permeating aspect of experience as class position.

APPENDIXES

APPENDIX A || FEATURES OF THE
CATALAN LANGUAGE

Classification. In the late nineteenth century, some philologists held that Catalan was a dialect of Occitan (or Languedoc or Provençal) (Sanchis Guarner 1980: 3). Since Catalonia was politically and culturally linked to Provence and other regions of Languedoc during the formative eleventh–thirteenth centuries, it is not surprising that there are linguistic links as well. It has been said that if all Romance languages are sisters, then Portuguese and Castilian are twins, and Catalan and Occitan are another set of twins (Coromines, quoted in ibid.: 17). Earlier in the present century, Iberian and German linguists attempted to group these languages into a diasystem of Gallic Latin and Hispanic Latin, placing Catalan in the Gallic rather than the Hispanic camp. Modern linguists have qualified this system as "a little byzantine" (ibid.: 20) and consider Catalan a transitional language between the groups, with the phonetic system and lexicon more closely related to the Gallic languages and the morphological system more Iberian.

Phonology and morphophonemics. Aurally, Catalan is quite dissimilar to Castilian. To many an unacquainted ear, it sounds more like Italian or Portuguese among the well-known Romance languages. Though there are several major dialects of Catalan, the following description is based on the Eastern Catalan dialect spoken in Barcelona, which has become a virtual oral standard.

Catalan has all the consonants of the Castilian phonemic inventory except the voiceless velar fricative /x/ and the voiceless interdental fricative /θ/. In addition, Catalan distinguishes the fricatives /z/, /ʃ/, and /ʒ/, and the affricate /ʤ/, which are not found in Castilian. These have given rise to tongue-twisters that are the bane of Castilians attempting to learn the language, e.g.,

Cat.: **Setze jutges d'un jutjat mengen fetge d'un penjat.**
/sedzə ʒudʒəz dun ʒudʒat mendʒən fedʒə dun pəndʒat/

Cast.: *Dieciseis jueces de un juzgado comen higado de un (hombre) colgado.*

'Sixteen judges from a court eat the liver of a hanged man.'

A geminate lateral, /ll/ (represented orthographically as 'l.l', e.g. in-tel.ligent, pel.licula), also has phonemic status in standard Catalan, with no analogue in Castilian. This phoneme is lost among most speakers, however, having merged with /l/.

The vowel system of Catalan is more complex than that of Castilian, with phonemic distinctions between "open" and "closed" versions of both 'o' and 'e' (/o/, /ɔ/; /e/, /ɛ/), e.g.,

net	/nɛt/	'clean'
nét	/net/	'grandson'
dóna	/'donə/	's/he gives'
dona	/'dɔnə/	'woman'

Catalan shares several phonological rules with Castilian; for example, voiced stops (b, d, g) become fricatives intervocalically (β, δ, ɣ). But it has several others rules that give Catalan a sound impression distinctive from Castilian. For example, /l/, especially after a back vowel, is velarized or dark: [ɫ]; this allophone is one of the more frequently remarked characteristics of a "Catalan accent."

An important phonological rule is that which reduces unstressed /a/, /e/, and /ɛ/ to schwa [ə], another phone not found in standard Castilian. Unstressed /o/ and /ɔ/ become [u]. Thus,

tot	[tot]	'everything'
total	[tu'tal]	'total'
obra	['o βrə]	'work'
obrer	[u'βre]	'worker'
contra	['kontrə]	'against'
contrari	[kun'trari]	'contrary'
carrer	[kə're]	'street'
carretera	[kərə'terə]	'road'
net	[nɛt]	'clean'
netejar	[nətə'ʒa]	'to clean'

These rules are often difficult for Castilian speakers to master, and a failure to reduce vowels often marks non-native Catalan speech.

Some phonemes present in both languages differ in their distribution. Both the palatal nasal /ɲ/ and lateral /ʎ/ are permitted, and even character-istic, in word-final position in Catalan, where they are not found in Castilian. Castilian speakers often find it difficult to produce these sounds in this en-vironment and may transform them to alveolars or an alveolar followed by a palatal glide.

any	[aɲ]	'year'
seny	[seɲ]	'sense'
lluny	[ʎuɲ]	'far'
ocell	[useʎ]	'bird'
treball	[trə'βaʎ]	'work'
ull	[uʎ]	'eye'

Liaison between words is obligatory in Catalan, giving rise to voicing of voiceless consonants, elision of vowels, and the pronunciation of word-final consonants that are unrealized before a consonant or in utterance-final position:

amb	[əm]	'with'
amb els altres	[əm bəl zaltrəs]	'with the others'
porta oberta	[pɔrt uβɛrtə]	'open door'
mig	[mitʃ]	'half'
mig any	[midʒ aɲ]	'half year'

Again, Castilians who learn Catalan often betray their non-native status by their nonmastery of the rules of liaison.

Catalan does not favor a canonical CV syllable structure as strongly as Castilian, and more word-final consonant clusters are permitted, e.g.:

tens	[tens]	'you have'
llarg	[ʎark]	'long'
disc	[disk]	'record'

Plurals may be formed by adding -s directly to a final consonant, which is not permitted in Castilian, e.g.:

Sing.	Plural	
gat	gats	'cats'
ocell	ocells	'birds'
disc	discs (alt.: discos)	'records'
gust	gusts (alt.: gustos)	'tastes'

Lexicon. There are many similarities between the lexicons of Catalan and Castilian. Both bilingual children and adult learners often deduce phonological rules to transform Castilian words to Catalan and vice versa. The best-known and most generally applied is the deletion of final vowels or consonants from Castilian to produce Catalan forms, e.g.:

Cast.	Cat.	
acción	acció	'action'
pan	pa	'bread'
disco	disc	'record'
gato	gat	'cat'
cuando	quan	'when'

propio	propi	'own'
cansado	cansat	'tired'

A learner can hit the desired target quite often by applying these transformational rules, but frequently they will result in a "barbarism" (an "incorrect" but commonly used form), or a completely unacceptable form, especially in the area of basic vocabulary. There are many anecdotes about learners (including this researcher) who overgeneralize the rules they have discerned.

The most important differences between the Castilian and Catalan lexicons derive from earlier and later Latin forms (Sanchis Guarner 1980: 15–16), e.g.:

Latin > Cast.	Latin > Cat.	
metus > *miedo*	pavore > **por**	'fear'
fervere > *hervir*	bullire > **bullir**	'boil'
rogare > *rogar*	pricare > **pregar**	'pray'
comedere > *comer*	manducare > **menjar**	'eat'
fabulare > *hablar*	parabolare > **parlar**	'talk'
salire > *salir*	surtire > **sortir**	'leave'
nata > *nada*	res > **res**	'nothing'
cama > *cama*	lectu > **llit**	'bed'

Other differences are said to derive from the influence of Germanic languages (ibid.: 24):

Cast.	Cat.	
loco	**boig**	'crazy'
rato	**estona**	'(short) time'
mejilla	**galta**	'cheek'

Catalan, like Castilian, distinguishes between two verbs corresponding to the English 'to be': **ser** (also **esser**) and **estar**. However, the semantic distinction is subtle, and usage does not correspond to that in Castilian; this has proved a ripe ground for interference, and the system has become confused. But generally, **estar** is not used to indicate location, as it is in Castilian, and is never used to give the location of inanimate objects. Thus, Cast. *Donde está la casa?* Cat.: **A on és la casa?** 'Where is the house?'

Syntax. Syntactically, Catalan is quite similar to Castilian in many respects, but distinctive features exist. The obligatory Catalan partitive clitic **en** (also orthographically represented as **'n** or **n'** depending on position) is similar to that of French, but has no counterpart in Castilian:

Cast.: *Quiero un poco más.* Cat.: **En vull una mica més.** 'I want a little more (of it).'

Use of the definite article with possessive adjectives is also obligatory in Catalan, but not permissible in Castilian:

Cast.: *mi padre, mi madre*   Cat.: **el meu pare, la meva mare** 'my father, my mother'

A complex system of pronominal clitics, too complicated to detail here, frustrates most learners of Catalan; weak pronouns each have several combining forms, depending on their position in a clause. The system varies considerably across dialect areas, and change is clearly proceeding in the direction of simplification.

As a final example of syntactic differences, Catalan has a periphrastic past tense that has no counterpart in Castilian. This tense is deceptively similar to the Castilian periphrastic future (which prescriptively does not exist in Catalan, though it has come into use). The Catalan past is formed by an inflected auxiliary plus the infinitive of the main verb; all but the first- and second-person plural forms of the auxiliary are identical to the present tense of the verb 'to go' (**anar**). In Castilian, by contrast, the future is formed from the conjugated 'to go' (*ir*) + *a* + infinitive. Thus:

Cast.: 'they go'   *van*
       'they are going to learn' *van a aprender*

Cat.: 'they go'   **van**
      'they learned'   **van aprendre**

Orthography. Castilian is well known as a language whose orthographic system matches quite closely its phonemic system. In Catalan, there is less of a one-to-one correspondence of sound to symbol. Schwa [ə] may be represented orthographically by 'a' or 'e'; [u] is represented by both 'u' and 'o'; [s] is variously represented as 's', 'ss', and 'ç'. Conversely, some orthographic symbols represent a variety of sounds, e.g.:

'x'	xarxa	[ʃarʃə]
	aixo	[əʃɔ]
	fixar	[fiksa]
	despatx	[dəspatʃ]
'g'	gust	[gust]
	lleig	[ʎetʃ]
	llarg	[ʎaɾk]
	sang	[saŋ]
	gener	[ʒəne]

These and other differences from Castilian conventions make reading and especially writing in Catalan an annoyingly error-ridden process for those with well-developed literacy skills in Castilian.

APPENDIX B ‖‖ MATCHED-GUISE TEXT

Euclides construyó su geometría, una geometría que resistió el paso de casi dos mil años, utilizando un método de trabajo especialmente acertado: el método axiomático. Euclides empezaba por enunciar una serie de verdades que le parecían evidentes por si mismas y que aceptaba sin demonstración previa. Por ejemplo, aceptaba que por dos puntos pasa siempre una recta, o que dos rectas no paralelas se cortan siempre en un solo punto. Una vez aceptados estos presupuestos básicos, las solas reglas del razonamiento le proporcionaban todo lo demás. A partir de los enunciados primitivos, los "axiomas," se iban encadenando una tras otra las deducciones que se desprendían de ellos; eran los "teoremas." Y a partir de los teoremas surgían cada vez más teoremas. La situación recordaba el brotar de las ramas de un árbol, o, para ser exactos, de varios árboles; a partir de unos troncos primigenios, los axiomas, se iban desgajando más y más ramas. Una misma rama puede estar conectada a otras varias. Ello significa que el teorema simbolizado por la rama se deduce de los teoremas que llegan hasta ella.

Por supuesto, la elección de los axiomas es en cierto sentido arbitraria; puede partirse de cierto conjunto de enunciados o de otro conjunto distinto. Lo único importante es que, aunque sea a partir de troncos distintos, y en posición posiblemente también distinta, aparezcan precisamente las mismas ramas. Quizá, lo que antes era una rama (un teorema), ahora sea un tronco (un axioma), y viceversa. Lo que en verdad importa es que se respeten las reglas deductivas y se mantenga el entramado en toda su complejidad.

Euclides va construir una geometria, una geometria que va resistir el pas de gairebé dos mil anys, utilitzant un mètode de treball especialment encertat: el mètode axiomàtic. Euclides comencava enunciant una sèrie de veritats que li semblaven evidents per elles mateixes i que acceptava sense demostració prèvia. Per exemple, acceptava que per dos punts passa sempre una recta, o que dues rectas no paral.leles es tallen sempre en un sol punt. Un cop acceptats aquests presupòsits bàsics, les soles regles del raonament li proporcionaven la resta. A partir dels enunciats primitius, els "axiomes", s'anaven encadenant una darrera l'altra les deduccions que se'n desprenien; eren els "teoremes". I a partir dels teoremes sorgien cada vegada més teoremes. La situació recordava la brotada de les branques d'un arbre, o, per ser més exactes, de diversos arbres; partint d'uns troncs primigenis, els axiomes, s'anaven desprenent més i més branques. Una mateixa branca pot estar conectada a d'altres de diferents. Això significa que el teorema simbolitzat per la branca es dedueix dels teoremes que arriben fins a ella.

Sens dubte, l'elecció dels axiomes és, en un cert sentit, arbitrària; es pot partir d'un cert conjunt d'enunciats o d'un altre conjunt diferent. L'única cosa important és que, encara que sigui a partir de troncs diferents, i en una posició possiblement diferent també, apareguin precisament les mateixes branques. Potser allò que abans era una branca (un teorema), ara sigui un tronc (un axioma) i viceversa. El que realment importa és que es respectin les regles deductives i es mantingui l'entramat en tota la seva complexitat.

Euclid constructed his geometry, a geometry that stood up to the passage of almost two thousand years, using an especially appropriate method: the axiomatic method. Euclid began by proposing a series of truths that seemed self-evident to him and which he accepted without prior proof. For example, he accepted the idea that only one line passes through two points, or that two lines that are not parallel always intersect each other at one single point. Once these basic assumptions were accepted, the rules of reasoning alone gave him all the rest. From these primitive propositions, the "axioms," the deductions that came from them took off one after the other; these were the "theorems." And from the theorems arose yet more theorems. The situation was like the budding of branches from a tree, or, to be more exact, from several trees. Starting from the trunks (the axioms), more and more branches grew out. One single branch can be connected to several others. That means that the theorem symbolized by the branch is deduced from the theorems that grow up to where it begins.

Of course, the choice of axioms is in some ways arbitrary; it can start from one particular set of propositions or from a different set. The only important thing is that the same branches appear, even though they may come from different trunks or perhaps in different positions. Perhaps what originally was a branch (a theorem) will now be a trunk (an axiom), and vice versa. What's really important is that the rules of deduction be respected and that the pattern be maintained in all its complexity.

APPENDIX C ‖‖ MATCHED-GUISE RESPONSE SHEET

CASTILIAN VERSION

La persona que habla,		Muy poco				Mucho	
A.	¿Te parece inteligente?	1	2	3	4	5	6
B.	¿Te parece simpática?	1	2	3	4	5	6
C.	¿Te parece una persona culta?	1	2	3	4	5	6
D.	¿Te parece que es atractiva físicamente?	1	2	3	4	5	6
E.	¿Te parece digna de confianza?	1	2	3	4	5	6
F.	¿Te parece que tiene sentido del humor?	1	2	3	4	5	6
G.	¿Te parece ambiciosa?	1	2	3	4	5	6
H.	¿Te parece una persona abierta?	1	2	3	4	5	6
I.	¿Te parece que tiene confianza en si misma?	1	2	3	4	5	6
J.	¿Te parece progresista?	1	2	3	4	5	6
K.	¿Te parece una persona generosa?	1	2	3	4	5	6
L.	¿Te parece capaz de dirigir?	1	2	3	4	5	6
M.	¿Te parece una persona divertida?	1	2	3	4	5	6
N.	¿Te parece una persona trabajadora?	1	2	3	4	5	6
O.	¿Te parece orgullosa?	1	2	3	4	5	6
P.	¿A qué tipo de trabajo piensas que se dedica?						

CATALAN VERSION

La persona qui parla,	Molt poc					Molt
A. Et sembla intel.ligent?	1	2	3	4	5	6
B. Et sembla simpàtica?	1	2	3	4	5	6
C. Et sembla una persona culta?	1	2	3	4	5	6
D. Et sembla que és atractiva físicament?	1	2	3	4	5	6
E. Et sembla digna de confiança?	1	2	3	4	5	6
F. Et sembla que té sentit de l'humor?	1	2	3	4	5	6
G. Et sembla ambiciosa?	1	2	3	4	5	6
H. Et sembla una persona oberta?	1	2	3	4	5	6
I. Et sembla que té confiança en ella mateixa? . .	1	2	3	4	5	6
J. Et sembla progressista?	1	2	3	4	5	6
K. Et sembla una persona generosa?	1	2	3	4	5	6
L. Et sembla capaç de dirigir?	1	2	3	4	5	6
M. Et sembla una persona divertida?	1	2	3	4	5	6
N. Et sembla una persona treballadora?	1	2	3	4	5	6
O. Et sembla orgullosa?	1	2	3	4	5	6
P. A quin tipus de feina penses que es dedica?						

APPENDIX D ||||| MATCHED-GUISE TEST,
RESPONDENT
PERSONAL DATA SHEET

CATALAN VERSION

A. 1. Edat
2. Sexe H D
3. Lloc de naixement   Província
4. Quan temps fa que vius a Catalunya?
5. Llengua que parles a casa: Castellà Català Les dues Altra
6. Llengua que parles amb els amics:
   Castellà Català Les dues Altra
7. Nivell d'estudis que estàs cursant
8. Nom de l'escola
9. Treballes? Sí No Tipus de feina
10. A què penses dedicar-te professionalment en el futur?

B. 1. Lloc de naixement del pare   Província
2. Ocupació del pare
3. Llengua que parla el pare a casa:
   Castellà Català Les dues Altra
4. Lloc de naixement de la mare   Província
5. Ocupació de la mare
6. Llengua que parla la mare a casa:
   Castellà Català Les dues Altra

C. Coneixements de català
1. L'entens?   Sí   Força   Poc   No
2. El parles?   Sí   Força   Poc   No
3. El llegeixes?   Sí   Força   Poc   No
4. L'escrius?   Sí   Força   Poc   No

D. Durant els teus estudis, en quina llengua es feien les classes?
    1. A la 1a etapa d'E.G.B.   Castellà   Català   Les dues
    2. A la 2a etapa d'E.G.B.   Castellà   Català   Les dues
    3. Al B.U.P./F.P.   Castellà   Català   Les dues
    4. Al C.O.U.   Castellà   Català   Les dues

CASTILIAN VERSION

A.   1. Edad
     2. Sexo   M F
     3. Lugar de nacimiento   Provincia
     4. Cuánto tiempo llevas en Cataluña?
     5. Lengua que hablas en casa: Castellano Catalán Las dos Otra
     6. Lengua que hablas con los amigos:
           Castellano Catalán Las dos Otra
     7. Nivel de estudios que estás realizando
     8. Nombre de la escuela
     9. Trabajas?   Sí No   Tipo de trabajo
    10. A qué piensas dedicarte profesionalmente en el futuro?

B.   1. Lugar de nacimiento del padre   Provincia
     2. Ocupación del padre
     3. Lengua que habla el padre en casa:
           Castellano Catalán Las dos Otra
     4. Lugar de nacimiento de la madre   Provincia
     5. Ocupación de la madre
     6. Lengua que habla la madre en casa:
           Castellano Catalán Las dos Otra

C.   Conocimientos de catalán
     1. Lo entiendes?   Sí   Bastante   Poco   No
     2. Lo hablas?   Sí   Bastante   Poco   No
     3. Lo lees?   Sí   Bastante   Poco   No
     4. Lo escribes?   Sí   Bastante   Poco   No

D.   Durante tus estudios, en qué lengua se impartían las clases?
     1. En 1a etapa de E.G.B.   Castellano   Catalán   Las dos
     2. En 2a etapa de E.G.B.   Castellano   Catalán   Las dos
     3. En B.U.P./F.P.   Castellano   Catalán   Las dos
     4. En C.O.U.   Castellano   Catalán   Las dos

ENGLISH TRANSLATION

A.   1. Age
     2. Sex   M F
     3. Birthplace   Province
     4. How long have you lived in Catalonia?

5. Language you speak at home: Castilian Catalan Both Other
6. Language you speak with your friends:
   Castilian Catalan Both Other
7. Your grade level
8. Name of school
9. Do you work?   Yes No Type of work
10. What kind of job would you like to have in the future?

B. 1. Father's birthplace   Province
    2. Father's occupation
    3. Language your father speaks at home:
       Castilian Catalan Both Other
    4. Mother's birthplace
    5. Mother's occupation
    6. Language your mother speaks at home:
       Castilian Catalan Both Other

C. Knowledge of Catalan

1. Do you understand it?	Yes	Pretty well	A little	No
2. Do you speak it?	Yes	Pretty well	A little	No
3. Do you read it?	Yes	Pretty well	A little	No
4. Do you write it?	Yes	Pretty well	A little	No

D. During your school years, in what language have classes been given?

1. Primary school (basic general education, 1st stage)	Castilian	Catalan	Both
2. Middle school (basic general education, 2d stage)	Castilian	Catalan	Both
3. High school (academic; technical)	Castilian	Catalan	Both
4. University preparatory course	Castilian	Catalan	Both

REFERENCES CITED

||| REFERENCES CITED

Alba, Victor. 1975. *Catalonia: A Profile*. New York: Praeger.
Allport, Gordon W., and H. Cantril. 1934. Judging personality from voice. *J. of Social Psychology* 5: 37–55.
Amelang, James S. 1986. *Honored Citizens of Barcelona: Patrician Culture and Class Relations, 1490–1714*. Princeton, N.J.: Princeton Univ. Press.
Aracil, Lluís V. 1982. *Papers de sociolingüística*. Barcelona: La Magrana.
Ardit, Manuel, Albert Balcells, and Núria Sales. 1980. *Història dels països catalans de 1714 a 1975*. Barcelona: EDHASA.
Argente, Joan. 1980. Un home d'una peça. *Avui*, June 8.
Argente, Joan, et al. 1979. Una nació sense estat, un poble sense llengua? *Els Marges* 15: 3–15.
Arnau, Joaquim. 1980. *Escola i contacte de llengües*. Barcelona: CEAC.
Arnau, Joaquim, and Humbert Boada. 1986. Languages and school in Catalonia. *J. Multilingual and Multicultural Development* 7(2–3): 107–22.
Avui. 1982. Situació de la llengua catalana. April 23.
Azevedo, Milton. 1984. The reestablishment of Catalan as a language of culture. *Hispanic Linguistics* 1(2): 305–30.
Badia i Margarit, Antoni M. 1969. *La llengua dels barcelonins*. Barcelona: Edicions 62.
Barceló, Miquel. 1978. La invasió àrab-musulmana i Catalunya. *L'Avenç* 7–8: 25–31.
Barth, Fredrik. 1969. Ethnic groups and boundaries. In F. Barth, ed., *Ethnic Groups and Boundaries*. Boston: Little, Brown. Pp. 9–38.

Bastardas i Boada, Albert. 1985. *La bilingüització de la segona generació immigrant: Realitat i factors a Vilafranca del Penedès.* Barcelona: La Magrana.

——. 1986. *Llengua i immigració: La segona generació immigrant a la Catalunya no-metropolitana.* Barcelona: La Magrana.

Benet, Josep. 1978. *Catalunya sota el règim franquista.* Barcelona: Editorial Blume.

Bloch, Marc. 1961. *Feudal Society,* Vols. 1 and 2. Chicago: Univ. Chicago Press.

Blom, Jan-Peter, and John J. Gumperz. 1972. Social meaning in linguistic structures: Code-switching in Norway. In J. Gumperz and D. Hymes, eds., *Directions in Sociolinguistics.* New York: Holt, Rinehart & Winston. Pp. 407–34.

Boix Selva, Emilio M. 1966. La condición social de los inmigrantes. *Estudios Geográficos* 27 (105): 547–60.

Bonnassie, Pierre. 1978. El feudalisme català; Segle onze. *L'Avenç* 7–8: 32–39.

Bourdieu, Pierre. 1977. *Outline of a Theory of Practice.* Cambridge: Cambridge Univ. Press.

——. 1982. *Ce que parler veut dire.* Paris: Fayard.

Bourdieu, Pierre, and Jean-Claude Passeron. 1977. *Reproduction in Education, Society and Culture.* London: Sage.

Bourhis, Richard Y. 1982. Language policies and language attitudes: Le monde de la francophonie. In E. B. Ryan and H. Giles, eds., *Attitudes Towards Language Variation: Social and Applied Contexts.* London: Edward Arnold. Pp. 34–62.

Bourhis, Richard Y., and Fred Genesee. 1980. Evaluative reactions to code switching strategies in Montreal. In H. Giles, W. P. Robinson, and P. M. Smith, eds., *Language: Social Psychological Perspectives.* Oxford: Pergamon. Pp. 335–43.

Bourhis, Richard Y., Howard Giles, and Wallace E. Lambert. 1975. Social consequences of accommodating one's speech style: A cross-national investigation. *International J. of Sociology of Language* 6: 55–72.

Brenan, Gerald. 1962. *The Spanish Labyrinth.* Cambridge: Cambridge Univ. Press.

Brown, Penelope, and Stephen Levinson. 1978. Universals in language usage: Politeness phenomena. In E. Goody, ed., *Questions and Politeness.* Cambridge: Cambridge Univ. Press. Pp. 56–289.

——. 1979. Social structure, groups and interaction. In K. R. Scherer and H. Giles, eds., *Social Markers in Speech.* Cambridge: Cambridge Univ. Press.

Brown, Roger, and Albert Gilman. 1960. Pronouns of power and solidarity. In Thomas Sebeok, ed., *Style in Language.* Cambridge, Mass.: MIT Press. Pp. 253–76.

Calsamiglia, Helena, and Amparo Tuson. 1980. Ús i alternança de llengües en grups de joves d'un barri de Barcelona. *Treballs de sociolingüística catalana* 3: 11–82.

Cambio 16. 1979. Andaluces en Cataluña: ¿Cataluces o andalanes? Sept. 16–22.

Candel, Francesc. 1964. *Els altres catalans.* Barcelona: Edicions 62.

———. 1977. Escriure en castellà a Catalunya. [Response to survey.] *Taula de canvi* 6: 16–17.

Caraben Ribó, A. 1982. Catalonia, an industrial country. In *Catalonia.* Barcelona: Generalitat de Catalunya. Pp. 81–87.

Carranza, Michael, and Ellen Bouchard Ryan. 1975. Evaluative reactions of bilingual Anglo and Mexican-American adolescents toward speakers of English and Spanish. *International J. of Sociology of Language* 6: 83–104.

Carter, Thomas P. 1970. *Mexican Americans in School: A History of Educational Neglect.* New York: College Entrance Examination Board.

Castellanos, Rafael. 1978. El debat sobre la integració dels immigrants a la societat catalana. *Quaderns d'Alliberament* 2–3: 173–230.

Clark, Robert P. 1980. Euzkadi: Basque nationalism in Spain since the Civil War. In C. R. Foster, ed., *Nations Without a State.* New York: Praeger. Pp. 75–100.

Cohen, Abner. 1974a. *Two-Dimensional Man.* Berkeley: Univ. California Press.

———. 1974b. Introduction: The lessons of ethnicity. In A. Cohen, ed., *Urban Ethnicity.* London: Tavistock. Pp. ix–xxiv.

Cole, Roger L. 1975. Divergent and convergent attitudes toward the Alsatian dialect. *Anthropological Linguistics* 17: 293–303.

Consell Executiu de la Generalitat de Catalunya. 1981. El Consell respeta y hace respetar los derechos lingüísticos de todos. In Direcció General de la Política Lingüística, *Por la normalización lingüística de Cataluña.* Barcelona: Generalitat de Catalunya. Pp. 18–19.

Cook-Gumperz, Jenny. 1981. Communication, language and social inequality in urban life. Paper presented at Annual Meeting of the American Anthropological Association, Los Angeles.

Cooper, Robert. 1978. The spread of Amhara in Ethiopia. In J. Fishman, ed., *Advances in the Study of Societal Multilingualism.* The Hague: Mouton. Pp. 459–76.

Cooper, Robert, and Joshua A. Fishman. 1974. The study of language attitudes. *International J. of Sociology of Language* 3: 5–19.

Cruells, Manuel. 1965. *Els no catalans i nosaltres.* Barcelona: Edicions d'aportació catalana.

Cummins, James. 1979. Linguistic interdependence and the educational development of bilingual children. *Review of Educational Research* 49: 222–51.

d'Anglejan, Alison, and G. Richard Tucker. 1973. Sociolinguistic correlates of speech style in Quebec. In R. Shuy and R. Fasold, eds., *Language Attitudes: Current Trends and Prospects.* Washington, D.C.: Georgetown Univ. Press. Pp. 1–27.

Despres, Leo A. 1975a. Ethnicity and ethnic group relations in Guyana. In J. W. Bennett, ed., *The New Ethnicity.* St. Paul, Minn.: West Publishing. Pp. 127–47.

————. 1975b. Ethnicity and resource competition in Guyanese society. In L. Despres, ed., *Ethnicity and Resource Competition in Plural Societies.* The Hague: Mouton. Pp. 86–117.

Deutsch, Karl W. 1966. *Nationalism and Social Communication.* 2d ed. Cambridge, Mass.: MIT Press.

DeVos, George. 1975. Ethnic pluralism: Conflict and accommodation. In G. DeVos and L. Romanucci-Ross, eds., *Ethnic Identity: Cultural Continuities and Change.* Palo Alto, Calif.: Mayfield. Pp. 5–41.

DiGiacomo, Susan. 1985. The politics of identity: Nationalism in Catalonia. Ann Arbor, Mich.: Univ. Microfilms International.

————. 1986. Images of class and ethnicity in Catalan politics, 1977–1980. In G. McDonogh, ed., *Conflict in Catalonia.* Gainesville: Univ. Florida Press. Pp. 72–92.

Dixon, Wilfred J., and Morton B. Brown, eds. 1977. *Biomedical Computer Programs P-Series.* Berkeley: Univ. California Press.

Dorian, Nancy. 1981. *Language Death.* Philadelphia: Univ. Pennsylvania Press.

Edelsky, Carole, et al. 1983. Semilingualism and language deficit. *Applied Linguistics* 4(1): 1–22.

El-Dash, Linda, and G. Richard Tucker. 1975. Subjective reactions to various speech styles in Egypt. *International J. of Sociology of Language* 6: 33–54.

Elliott, J. H. 1963. *The Revolt of the Catalans: A Study in the Decline of Spain (1598–1640).* Cambridge: Cambridge Univ. Press.

Esteva Fabregat, C. 1973. Inmigración, etnicidad y relaciones interétnicas en Barcelona. *Ethnica* 6: 73–129.

————. 1974. Aculturación lingüística de inmigrados en Barcelona. *Ethnica* 8: 73–120.

————. 1976. Consciencia étnica y consciencia de clase: El caso de Cataluña. *Estudios Regionales.* Madrid: Instituto Nacional de Progreso y Desarollo. Pp. 385–90.

————. 1978. Immigració i confirmació ètnica a Barcelona. *Quaderns d'Alliberament* 2–3: 47–80.

Evans-Pritchard, E. E. 1940. *The Nuer.* Oxford: Oxford Univ. Press.

Fishman, Joshua A. 1964. Language maintenance and language shift as a field of inquiry. *Linguistics* 9: 32–70.

————. 1967. Bilingualism with and without diglossia; diglossia with and without bilingualism. *J. of Social Issues* 23(2): 29–38.

————. 1972a. *Language in Sociocultural Change.* Stanford, Calif.: Stanford Univ. Press.

————. 1972b. *Language and Nationalism: Two Integrative Essays.* Rowley, Mass.: Newbury House.

————. 1972c. The sociology of language. In P. Giglioli, ed., *Language and Social Context.* Harmondsworth, Eng.: Penguin. Pp. 45–58.

Fox, Richard G., Charlotte Aull, and Louis Cimino. 1978. Ethnic nationalism and political mobilization in industrial societies. In E. Ross, ed., *Interethnic Communication.* Athens: Univ. Georgia Press. Pp. 113–33.

Gaines, Atwood. 1978. The word and the cross. Unpublished Ph.D. dissertation, Department of Anthropology, Univ. California, Berkeley.

Gal, Susan. 1978. Peasant men can't get wives: Language change and sex roles in a bilingual community. *Language in Society* 7: 1–16.

———. 1979. *Language Shift*. New York: Academic Press.

Gans, Herbert J. 1962. *The Urban Villagers*. New York: Free Press.

———. 1972. The working class, lower class and middle class. In R. Abrahams and R. Troike, eds., *Language and Cultural Diversity in American Education*. Englewood Cliffs, N.J.: Prentice-Hall. Pp. 47–55.

García Cárcel, Ricardo. 1987. El concepte d'Espanya als segles xvi i xvii. *L'Avenç* 100: 38–51.

Gardner, Robert C., and Wallace E. Lambert. 1972. *Attitudes and Motivation in Second-Language Learning*. Rowley, Mass.: Newbury House.

Geertz, Clifford. 1973. *The Interpretation of Cultures*. New York: Basic Books.

Generalitat de Catalunya. 1980. Declaració del Consell Executiu sobre normalització del català. Barcelona.

Giles, Howard. 1970. Evaluative reactions to accents. *Educational Review* 22: 211–27.

———. 1973. Accent mobility: A model and some data. *Anthropological Linguistics* 15: 87–105.

Giles, Howard, and Peter F. Powesland. 1975. *Speech Style and Social Evaluation*. New York: Academic Press.

Giles, Howard, Donald M. Taylor, and Richard Y. Bourhis. 1973. Towards a theory of interpersonal accommodation through language: Some Canadian data. *Language in Society* 2: 177–92.

Giner, Salvador. 1984. *The Social Structure of Catalonia*. 2d ed. Sheffield: The Anglo-Catalan Society.

Grama. 1979. Volveré a Santa Coloma cuando me lo pidan otra vez. May 16–26.

Grillo, R. D. 1980. Introduction. In R. Grillo, ed., *"Nation" and "State" in Europe*. New York: Academic Press. Pp. 1–30.

Guardiola, Carles-Jordi. 1980. *Per la llengua. Llengua i cultura als Països Catalans, 1939–1977*. Barcelona: La Magrana.

Gumperz, John J. 1958. Dialect differences and social stratification in a North Indian village. *American Anthropologist* 60: 668–82.

———. 1962. Types of linguistic communities. *Anthropological Linguistics* 4(1): 28–40.

———. 1971. *Language in Social Groups*. Stanford, Calif.: Stanford Univ. Press.

———. 1972. The speech community. In P. Giglioli, ed., *Language and Social Context*. Harmondsworth, Eng.: Penguin. Pp. 219–31.

———. 1982. *Discourse Strategies*. Cambridge: Cambridge Univ. Press.

Gumperz, John J., and Eduardo Hernandez-Chavez. 1978. Bilingualism, bidialectalism, and classroom interaction. In M. Lowrie and N. Conklin, eds., *A Pluralistic Nation*. Rowley, Mass.: Newbury House. Pp. 275–94.

Gumperz, John J., and Robert Wilson. 1971. Convergence and creolization:

A case from the Indo-Aryan/Dravidian border in India. In D. Hymes, ed., *Pidginization and Creolization of Languages*. London: Cambridge Univ. Press. Pp. 151–67.

Hammel, Eugene A. 1969. *Power in Ica*. Boston: Little, Brown.

Hansen, Edward C. 1977. *Rural Catalonia Under the Franco Regime*. Cambridge: Cambridge Univ. Press.

Haugen, Einar. 1972. *The Ecology of Language*. Stanford, Calif.: Stanford Univ. Press.

Hechter, Michael. 1975. *Internal Colonialism: The Celtic Fringe in British National Development, 1536–1966*. Berkeley: Univ. California Press.

Heiberg, Marianne. 1980. Basques, Anti-Basques and the moral community. In R. Grillo, ed., *"Nation" and "State" in Europe*. New York: Academic Press. Pp. 45–60.

Heller, Monica S. 1982. Negotiations of language choice in Montreal. In J. Gumperz, ed., *Language and Social Identity*. Cambridge: Cambridge Univ. Press. Pp. 108–18.

Inglehart, R. F., and M. Woodward. 1972. Language conflicts and political community. In P. Giglioli, ed., *Language and Social Context*. Harmondsworth, Eng.: Penguin. Pp. 358–77.

Isaacs, Harold R. 1975. *Idols of the Tribe*. New York: Harper and Row.

Iverson, Gudmund N., and Helmut Norpoth. 1976. *Analysis of Variance: Quantitative Applications in the Social Sciences*, Vol. 1. Beverly Hills, Calif.: Sage.

Jackson, Gabriel. 1965. *The Second Republic and the Spanish Civil War*. Princeton, N.J.: Princeton Univ. Press.

Jiménez Losantos, Federico. 1979. *Lo que queda de España*. Zaragoza: Alcrudo.

Jones, Norman. 1984. Regionalism and revolution in Catalonia. In P. Preston, ed., *Revolution and War in Spain*. London: Methuen. Pp. 85–112.

Junyent, Rosa. 1979. L'ús de la llengua catalana. *Avui*, March 18.

Jutglar, Antoni. 1971. *Ideologías y clases en la España contemporánea: 1874–1931*, Vol. 2. Madrid: EDICUSA.

Kern, Robert W. 1978. *Red Years, Black Years: A Political History of Spanish Anarchism, 1911–1937*. Philadelphia: ISHI.

Kim, Jae-On. 1975. Factor analysis. In N. Nie et al., *Statistical Package for the Social Sciences*. 2d ed. New York: McGraw-Hill.

Kim, Jae-On, and Charles W. Mueller. 1978. *Introduction to Factor Analysis: Quantitative Applications in the Social Sciences*, Vol. 13. Beverly Hills, Calif.: Sage.

Kloss, Heinz. 1966. Types of multilingual communities: A discussion of ten variables. *Sociological Inquiry* 36: 135–45.

———. 1967a. Bilingualism and nationalism. *J. of Social Issues* 23 (2): 39–47.

———. 1967b. "Abstand" languages and "ausbau" languages. *Anthropological Linguistics* 9 (7): 29–41.

Labov, William. 1966a. *The Social Stratification of English in New York City*. Washington, D.C.: Center for Applied Linguistics.

————. 1966b. Hypercorrection by the lower middle class as a factor in linguistic change. In W. Bright, ed., *Sociolinguistics*. The Hague: Mouton. Pp. 84–113.

————. 1972. *Sociolinguistic Patterns*. Philadelphia: Univ. Pennsylvania.

————. 1973. On the linguistic consequences of being a lame. *Language in Society* 2: 81–115.

Lambert, Wallace E. 1967. A social psychology of bilingualism. *J. of Social Issues* 23: 91–109.

Lambert, Wallace E., Howard Giles, and Omer Picard. 1975. Language attitudes in a French-American community. *International J. of Sociology of Language* 4: 127–52.

Lambert, Wallace E., Richard C. Hodgson, Richard C. Gardner, and Samuel Fillenbaum. 1960. Evaluational reactions to spoken languages. *Journal of Abnormal and Social Psychology* 60(1): 44–51.

Leman, Jordi. 1979. Carta oberta al meu fillol. *Avui*, Nov. 17.

Lewis, E. Glyn. 1978. Types of bilingual communities. In J. Alatis, ed., *Georgetown University Round Table on Languages and Linguistics 1978*. Washington, D.C.: Georgetown Univ. Press. Pp. 19–34.

Linz, Juan J. 1973. Early state building and late peripheral nationalism against the state: The case of Spain. In S. Eisenstadt and S. Rokkan, eds., *Building States and Nations*. Beverly Hills, Calif.: Sage. Pp. 32–116.

————. 1975. Politics in a multi-lingual society with a dominant world language: The case of Spain. In J.-G. Savard and R. Vigneault, eds., *Multilingual Political Systems: Problems and Solutions*. Quebec: Laval Univ. Press. Pp. 367–444.

Linz, Juan J., and Amando de Miguel. 1966. Within-nation differences and comparisons: The eight Spains. In R. Merrit and S. Rokkan, eds., *Comparing Nations: The Use of Quantitative Data in Cross-National Research*. New Haven, Conn.: Yale Univ. Press. Pp. 267–319.

López del Castillo, Lluís. 1976. *Llengua standard i nivells de llenguatge*. Barcelona: Laia.

Macauley, Ronald. 1973. Double standards. *American Anthropologist* 75(5): 1324–37.

Maluquer Sostres, Joaquim. 1963. *L'assimilation des immigrés en Catalogne*. Geneva: Librairie Droz.

————. 1966. Aspectos de la asimilación cultural de los inmigrados. *Estudios geográficos* 27(105): 553–641.

Martínez Shaw, Carles. 1978. Catalunya i els Borbons al segle xviii. *L'Avenç* 7–8: 50–55.

McDonogh, Gary. 1981. Elite language shift in Catalonia. Paper presented at the Forum for Interdisciplinary Research, Cancún.

————. 1986a. *Good Families of Barcelona: A Social History of Power in the Industrial Era*. Princeton, N.J.: Princeton Univ. Press.

————. 1986b. Introduction: Urban models and urban conflicts. In G. McDonogh, ed., *Conflict in Catalonia*. Gainesville: Univ. Florida Press. Pp. 1–16.

————. 1986c. A night at the opera: Imagery, patronage and conflict, 1840–

1940. In G. McDonogh, ed., *Conflict in Catalonia*. Gainesville, Univ. Florida Press. Pp. 33–53.

Medina, Manuel. 1975. Spain: Regional, linguistic and ideological conflict. In W. Veenhoven, ed., *Case Studies in Human Rights and Fundamental Freedoms: A World Survey*. The Hague: Martinus Nijhoff. Pp. 135–54.

Miguel, Amando de, et al. 1981. Manifiesto: Por la igualdad de derechos lingüísticos en Cataluña. March 12. Madrid: *Diario 16*, Disidencias 17.

Milroy, Lesley. 1980. *Language and Social Networks*. Oxford: Basil Blackwell.

Mitchell, J. Clyde. 1974. Perceptions of ethnicity and ethnic behavior: An empirical exploration. In A. Cohen, ed., *Urban Ethnicity*. London: Tavistock. Pp. 1–36.

Moll, Aina. 1981. La situación sociolingüística en Cataluña. In *Por la normalización lingüística de Cataluña*. Barcelona: Generalitat de Catalunya. Pp. 12–13.

Moore, Sally Falk. 1975. Epilogue: Uncertainties in situations, indeterminacies in culture. In S. Moore and B. Meyerhoff, eds., *Symbol and Politics in Communal Ideology*. Ithaca, N.Y.: Cornell Univ. Press. Pp. 210–39.

Mougeon, Raymond, and Edouard Beniak. 1989. Language contraction and linguistic change: The case of Welland French. In N. Dorian, ed., *Investigating Obsolescence: Studies in Language Contraction and Death*. Cambridge: Cambridge Univ. Press.

Mundo Diario. 1979. Quieren seguir siendo españoles. Nov. 28.

Murray, Stephen. 1981. Gatekeepers' shared procedures and the disproportionate elimination of Asian-American applicants. Paper presented to the Annual Meeting of the American Anthropological Association, Los Angeles.

Nadal, Josep M. 1987. El català en els segles xvi i xvii. *L'Avenç* 100: 24–31.

Nadal i Oller, Jordi. 1987. L'economia catalana en el marc de l'economia espanyola: Catalunya, la fàbrica d'Espanya (1833–1936). In J. Fontana et al., *Catalunya i Espanya al segle xix*. Barcelona: Columna. Pp. 59–78.

Nie, Norman H., C. Hadlai Hull, Jean G. Jenkins, Karin Steinbrenner, and Dale H. Bent. 1975. *Statistical Package for the Social Sciences*. 2d ed. New York: McGraw-Hill.

Ninyoles, Rafael Ll. 1976. *Bases per a una política lingüística democràtica a l'estat espanyol*. València: Quaderns Tres i Quatre.

Novak, Michael. 1980. Pluralism in humanistic perspective. In W. Peterson et al., *Concepts of Ethnicity*. Cambridge, Mass.: Harvard Univ. Press. Pp. 27–56.

Ogbu, John. 1978. *Minority Education and Caste*. New York: Academic Press.

Orridge, A. W. 1982. Separatist and autonomist nationalisms: The structure of regional loyalties in the modern state. In C. Williams, ed., *National Separatism*. Vancouver: Univ. British Columbia Press. Pp. 43–74.

Ortega y Gasset, José. 1936. *Obras de José Ortega y Gasset*. 2d ed. Madrid: Espasa-Calpe.

Ortner, Sherry B. 1973. On key symbols. *American Anthropologist* 75(5): 1338–46.

Orwell, George. 1952. *Homage to Catalonia*. New York: Harcourt, Brace, Jovanovich. [First published 1938.]

Osgood, Charles E. 1964. Semantic differential techniques in the comparative study of cultures. *American Anthropologist* 66(3): 171–200.

Osgood, Charles E., George J. Suci, and Percy H. Tannenbaum. 1957. *The Measurement of Meaning*. Urbana: Univ. Illinois Press.

Pedrolo, Manuel de, et al. 1981. *Quan cal, hi som tots!* Barcelona: Diafora.

Pinilla de las Heras, Esteban. 1979. *Estudios sobre cambio social y estructuras sociales en Cataluña*. Madrid: Centro de Investigaciones Sociológicas.

Pi-Sunyer, Oriol. 1977. The maintenance of ethnic identity in Catalonia. In O. Pi-Sunyer, ed., *The Limits of Integration*. Amherst: Univ. Massachusetts Press. Pp. 111–46.

———. 1978. The 1977 parliamentary elections in Barcelona: Primordial sentiments in a time of change. Paper presented at the Conference on Ethnicity and Economic Development: East and West. Ann Arbor, Mich.

———. 1980. Dimensions of Catalan nationalism. In C. Foster, ed., *Nations Without a State*. New York: Praeger. Pp. 101–15.

Poplack, Shana. 1980. Sometimes I'll start a sentence in English *y termino en español*: Towards a typology of codeswitching. *Linguistics* 18: 581–618.

Prat de la Riba, Enric. 1978. *La nacionalitat catalana*. Barcelona: Edicions 62. [First published 1906.]

Recolons, Lluís, et al. 1979. *Catalunya: Home i territori*. Barcelona: Editorial Blume.

Reixach, Modest. 1975. *La llengua del poble*. Barcelona: Nova Terra.

———. 1985. Coneixement i ús de la llengua catalana a la província de Barcelona. Barcelona: Departament de Cultura de la Generalitat de Catalunya.

Riquer, Borja de. 1987a. Els corrents conservadors catalans i la seva evolució cap al catalanisme polític. *L'Avenç* 100: 78–85.

———. 1987b. La vida política catalana (1856–1898). In J. Fontana et al., *Catalunya i Espanya al segle xix*. Barcelona: Columna. Pp. 19–58.

Roberts, Catrin, and Glyn Williams. 1980. Attitudes and ideological bases of support for Welsh as a minority language. In H. Giles, W. Robinson, and P. Smith, eds., *Language: Social Psychological Perspectives*. Oxford: Pergamon. Pp. 227–32.

Roca, Encarna. 1977. *Qui és català*. Barcelona: Dopesa.

Rodriguez, Richard. 1981. *Hunger of Memory*. New York: David Godine.

Rokkan, Stein. 1972. Models and methods in the comparative study of nation-building. In T. Nossiter, A. Hanson, and S. Rokkan, eds., *Imagination and Precision in the Social Sciences*. New York: Humanities Press.

Rubin, Joan. 1968. Bilingual usage in Paraguay. In J. Fishman, ed., *Readings in the Sociology of Language*. The Hague: Mouton. Pp. 512–30.

Ryan, Ellen Bouchard. 1979. Why do low-prestige language varieties persist? In H. Giles and R. St. Clair, eds., *Language and Social Psychology*. Oxford: Basil Blackwell. Pp. 145–57.

Ryan, Ellen Bouchard, and M. A. Carranza. 1977. Ingroup and outgroup reactions to Mexican American language varieties. In H. Giles, ed., *Language, Ethnicity and Intergroup Relations*. London: Academic Press. Pp. 59–82.

Sáez, Armand. 1980. Catalunya, gresol o explotadora? Notes sobre immigració i creixement. In J. Ainaud et al., *Immigració i reconstrucció nacional a Catalunya*. Barcelona: Editorial Blume. Pp. 25–42.

Salrach, Josep M. 1978. La independència de Catalunya; segles ix–x. *L'Avenç* 7–8: 25–31.

Sanchis Guarner, Manuel. 1980. *Aproximació a la història de la llengua catalana*. Barcelona: Salvat.

Sellares, Miquel. 1980. Construir Catalunya sin electoralismos. *Mundo Diario*, June 12.

Shabad, Goldie, and Richard Gunther. 1982. Language, nationalism and political conflict in Spain. *Comparative Politics* (July): 443–77.

Shils, Edward. 1957. Primordial, personal, sacred and civil ties. *British J. of Sociology* 8: 130–45.

Simmel, Georg. 1950. *The Sociology of Georg Simmel*. Ed. and tr. K. H. Wolff. New York: Free Press.

Skuttnabb-Kangas, Tove. 1979. Language in the process of cultural assimilation and structural incorporation of linguistic minorities. Roslyn, Va.: National Clearinghouse for Bilingual Education.

Skuttnabb-Kangas, Tove, and Pertti Toukomaa. 1976. *Teaching Migrant Children's Mother Tongue and Learning the Language of the Host Country in the Context of the Socio-Cultural Situation of the Migrant Family*. Helsinki: Finnish National Commission for UNESCO.

Smith, M. G. 1960. Social and cultural pluralism. *New York Academy of Sciences Annals* 83(5): 763–85.

Smith, Philip H., Howard Giles, and Miles Hewstone. 1978. Sociolinguistics: A social psychological perspective. In R. St. Clair and H. Giles, eds., *Social and Psychological Contexts of Language*. Hillsdale, N.J.: Erlbaum. Pp. 13–22.

Sobrequés i Callicó, Jaume. 1987. La corona d'Aragó o confederació catalano-aragonesa: Els origens, segle xii. *L'Avenç* 100: 14–21.

Solé, Carlota. 1980. La "catalanització" dels immigrats. *Taula de Canvi* 20: 13–41.

———. 1982. *Los inmigrantes en la sociedad y en la cultura catalanas*. Barcelona: Ediciones Península.

———. 1987. Articulació social i cultural. In S. Aguilar et al., *Visió de Catalunya: El canvi i la reconstrucció nacional des de la perspectiva sociològica*. Barcelona: Diputació de Barcelona. Pp. 321–30.

Solé, Carlota, and Jesús Vicens. 1979. Integració, assimilació, explotació . . . ? *Perspectiva social* 14: 35–91.

Solé-Tura, Jordi. 1974. *Catalanismo i revolución burguesa*. Madrid: EDI-CUSA.

Stewart, William A. 1968. A sociolinguistic typology for describing national multilingualism. In J. Fishman, ed., *Readings in the Sociology of Language*. The Hague: Mouton. Pp. 531–45.

Stieblich, Christel. 1986. Interpersonal accommodation in a bilingual setting. *Language Planning and Language Policy* 10 (2): 158–76.

Strubell i Trueta, Miquel. 1978. Immigració i assimilació lingüística al Principat. *Quaderns d'Alliberament* 2–3: 241–57.

———. 1980. Crisi del concepte d'identitat [letter to the editor]. *Avui*, Nov. 17.

———. 1981a. La situació actual de la llengua catalana. Unpublished manuscript.

———. 1981b. *Llengua i població a Catalunya*. Barcelona: La Magrana.

Subirats, Marina. 1980. La utilització del català: Entre la precarietat i la normalització. *Saber* 1: 34–50.

Taylor, Philip. 1983. *Public Power in Catalonia*. Houston, Tex.: American Institute for Catalan Studies.

Termes, Josep. 1983. La immigració a Catalunya: Política i cultura. In P. Vilar et al., *Reflexions crítiques sobre la cultura catalana*. Barcelona: Departament de Cultura de la Generalitat de Catalunya. Pp. 199–315.

———. 1987. Corrents de pensament i d'acció del moviment catalanista. In J. Fontana et al., *Catalunya i Espanya al segle xix*. Barcelona: Columna. Pp. 177–87.

Tilly, Charles. 1975. Reflections on the history of European state-making. In C. Tilly, ed., *The Formation of National States in Western Europe*. Princeton, N.J.: Princeton Univ. Press. Pp. 3–83.

Timm, L. A. 1975. Spanish-English codeswitching: *El porqué y* how-not-to. *Romance Philology* 28 (4): 473–82.

Torres, Joaquim. 1977. Les enquestes sociolingüístiques catalanes. *Treballs de sociolingüística catalana* 1: 137–46.

———. 1980. La immigració i la llengua catalana: documentació sobre coneixements, usos i actituds lingüístics. In J. Ainaud et al., *Immigració i reconstrucció nacional a Catalunya*. Barcelona: Editorial Blume. Pp. 43–58.

Troike, Rudolph C. 1978. Research evidence for the effectiveness of bilingual education. *Bilingual Education Paper Series* 2 (5). Los Angeles: National Dissemination and Assessment Center.

Trudgill, Peter. 1972. Sex, covert prestige and linguistic change in the urban British English of Norwich. *Language in Society* 1: 179–96.

Tucker, G. Richard, and Wallace E. Lambert. 1969. White and Negro listeners' reactions to various American-English dialects. *Social Forces* 47: 463–68.

Ullman, Joan Connelly. 1968. *The Tragic Week: A Study of Anticlericalism in Spain, 1875–1912*. Cambridge, Mass.: Harvard Univ. Press.

Vallverdú, Francesc. 1979. *La normalització lingüística a Catalunya*. Barcelona: Laia.

———. 1980. *Aproximació crítica a la sociolingüística catalana.* Barcelona: Edicions 62.

Veny, Joan. 1986. *Els parlars catalans.* 6th ed. Palma de Mallorca: Editorial Moll.

Verdery, Katherine. 1983. *Transylvanian Villagers.* Berkeley: Univ. California Press.

Verdoodt, A. 1972. The differential impact of immigrant French speakers on indigenous German speakers. In J. Fishman, ed., *Advances in the Sociology of Language,* Vol. 2. The Hague: Mouton. Pp. 377–85.

Vicens Vives, Jaume. 1958. *Industrials i polítics del segle xix.* Barcelona: Vicens Vives.

Vilar, Pierre. 1979a. *Catalunya dins l'Espanya moderna.* Barcelona: Edicions 62. [First French edition 1962.]

———. 1979b. *Assaigs sobre la Catalunya del segle xviii.* Barcelona: Curial.

Vinyals i Soler, Ramon. 1980a. Ser o no ser catalán. *Mundo Diario,* June 12.

———. 1980b. Un cierto patriotismo. *Mundo Diario,* June 26.

Weber, Max. 1958. *From Max Weber: Essays in Sociology.* Tr. and ed. H. Gerth and C. Mills. New York: Oxford Univ. Press.

Webster's New Collegiate Dictionary. 1960. Springfield, Mass.: G. & C. Merriam.

Weinreich, Uriel. 1974. *Languages in Contact.* The Hague: Mouton. [1st ed. 1954.]

White, Geoffrey. 1980. Conceptual universals in interpersonal language. *American Anthropologist* 82(4): 759–92.

Wolck, Wolfgang. 1973. Attitudes toward Spanish and Quechua in bilingual Peru. In R. Shuy and R. Fasold, eds., *Language Attitudes.* Washington, D.C.: Georgetown Univ. Press. Pp. 129–47.

Woolard, Kathryn A. 1982. The problem of linguistic prestige: Evidence from Catalonia. *Penn Review of Linguistics* 6: 82–89.

———. 1984. A formal measure of language attitudes in Barcelona. *International J. of Sociology of Language* 47: 63–71.

———. 1985a. Language variation and cultural hegemony: Toward an integration of sociolinguistic and social theory. *American Ethnologist* 12(4): 738–48.

———. 1985b. Catalonia: The dilemma of language rights. In N. Wolfson and J. Manes, eds., *Language of Inequality.* The Hague: Mouton. Pp. 91–109.

———. 1986a. The politics of language status planning: "Normalization" in Catalonia. In N. Schweda-Nicholson, ed., *Language in the International Perspective.* Norwood, N.J.: Ablex. Pp. 91–102.

———. 1986b. The "crisis in the concept of identity" in contemporary Catalonia, 1976–82. In G. McDonogh, ed., *Conflict in Catalonia: Images of Urban Society.* Gainesville: Univ. Florida Press. Pp. 54–71.

———. 1987. Comedy and codeswitching in Catalonia. *Papers in Pragmatics* 1(1): 106–22.

———. 1988. Language convergence and language death as social processes. In N. Dorian, ed., *Investigating Obsolescence: Studies in Language Contraction and Death*. Cambridge: Cambridge Univ. Press.

Zentella, Ana Celia. 1981. Tá bien, you could answer me *en cualquier idioma*. In R. Duran, ed., *Latino Language and Communicative Behavior*. Norwood, N.J.: Ablex. Pp. 109–32.

INDEX

⦀ INDEX